BLAMELESS

Living a Life Free from
Guilt and Shame

BLAMELESS

Living a Life Free from Guilt and Shame

CHRISTY FITZWATER

Foreword by Lisa Jacobson
of Club31Women.com

LOYAL
ARTS MEDIA

Published by
Loyal Arts Media
P.O. Box 1414
Bend, OR 97709
loyalartsmedia.com

Printed in the United States of America

Cover Design by Darlene Schacht

ISBN 978-1-929125-44-9 (paperback)

Table of Contents

FOREWORD

I know now that it was a mistake.

But how could I have known it back then?

It actually seemed like a nice idea at the time. I would drive into town, settle into one of my favorite coffee shops (where they serve the most amazing homemade tiny donuts), order a 16 oz. latte for "here," and spend the rest of the afternoon reading Christy's new manuscript.

Doesn't that sound like a good idea to you?

Yes, that's what I thought too.

Except it didn't exactly go as planned.

I anticipated a quiet read through the smallish stack of papers, but it didn't turn out like that. Not at all. Three pages into it I began laughing aloud - which can be a rather embarrassing experience when you're in such a public place. What's more, this was the kind of café that business people go to in order to get their work done. It's for serious stuff.

Not for laughing.

And besides, I was sitting *alone* and that made it three times as mortifying.

But not as bad as it could get. Because it's even worse when you try to stifle your laughter and it sneaks out into something of a snort. And the powder sugar dusting on your tiny donuts blows everywhere.

That's definitely worse.

You'll be glad to hear though that I eventually gained some composure, read a few more pages, and soon found myself lost in the majestic mountains of Montana where Christy lives. In fact, I became so caught up in her story that I was convinced I was sitting right there sipping my coffee at her kitchen table. Feeling her remorse. Rejoicing at her small victories. Nodding my head through each chapter.

Christy might not have realized it, but I could relate to it all. In my own way and in my own circumstances. But I found myself—my story—right there on every page.

So you can see that things were now going quite well in my afternoon reading. That is until I got to that one unexpected part and I found myself suddenly crying. Tears-flowing-down-my-cheeks crying. Why-is-she-bawling-in-this-café crying. Weeping big tears over those tiny homemade donuts.

And, of course, wouldn't you know it, my husband decided, at that very moment, to call and check in on me, and I answered with a disturbingly choked up "hellooooo." It took quite a while to reassure him that I hadn't been in a car accident after all. *It's just that it was so sad and so sweet and so true....* Poor man, what he goes through.

Then I popped another one of those tiny donuts in my mouth (I did mention that they were *tiny*, right?) to cheer myself up and went on to the next chapter. I simply couldn't stop there.

Would you believe me if I told you that I've never read a book quite like this?

It's true. Reading Christy's book is like you're talking to one of your dearest friends. She is funny and honest and vulnerable and wise—all at the same time. And when you're done reading, you feel like you've known her for your entire life. Almost as if you grew up together in the same hometown. Shared secrets and adventures, failures and successes, joys and sorrows. It's like you've somehow grown up together.

Because this book isn't only about Christy. I mean, it is and it isn't.

It's also about me and it's about you.

And how we know we mess up and sometimes wonder if we're ever going to get this thing right. Our life, our home, our relationships, and everything in between. And all of it weighs us down.

We silently question if there's any real hope for us?

And there is.

You might find it hard to believe, but your life is overflowing with hope. You are on your way to becoming holy and good and all that you ever wanted to be.

You—yes, *you*—can live a beautiful life free of guilt and shame.

You, my friend, can be blameless.

Just ask Christy and she'll tell you...

Lisa Jacobson
Club31Women.com

CHAPTER ONE

FOR YOU WHO FALL SHORT OF PERFECTION

It starts with a flannel-covered pillow, because when you live an hour south of the Canadian border in a house nestled up against the Rocky Mountains, you need flannel sheets for nine and a half months of the year.

My son and I agree that a person's head should sink into a pillow. Not that flat, unfluffable, polyester imposter that sits on my husband's side of the bed.

"Hand me my pillow," my husband says.

"Oh, you mean this piece of cardboard slipped into a pillowcase? Is that what you're talking about?" I say.

"Yeah, not that huge thing that's so big your chin

touches your chest when you sleep," he replies.

If you're going to argue with your husband about the same topic for twenty-some years, then make sure it's over something like pillows.

My head sinks into my flannel-encased down pillow every night. It sinks so deeply that I have to use my hand to create a tunnel so I can breathe. I get cozy under the covers, but then my mind starts walking back through the day.

Losing the effect of the flannel goodness, I mentally replay all the fails. I think about the conversation in which I should have kept my mouth shut, or at least should have said something different. I think about the Wendy's wrappers in the garbage, and how there should have been leftovers from a homemade meal in the fridge instead. I remember that I should have called a church friend, to see if she was feeling better, but I didn't. My stomach churns with anxiety over my shortcomings. Paul says, "For all have sinned and fall short of the glory of God" (Romans 3:23), and there is no need to argue with him when I know I fall short every day.

There are times I've gotten up out of bed, restless. I've gone downstairs and sat by my husband on the couch, because he is the late-nighter of the two.

"What's the matter, Honey?" he asks. And even

though he's a Baptist preacher with no ecclesiastical collar, I unload on him all the stories of how I messed up during the day. I moan. He hugs and consoles me. He tells me I am not the biggest loser on the entire planet Earth, or maybe even in the Milky Way. But in all his skilled listening, he cannot repair the day. What I need is a place to rest my head.

I didn't really think twenty sentences was that big a deal. My freshman Spanish students had already learned a nice chunk of vocabulary, and they had done the tedious work of making a special reference book full of fifty useful verbs, each conjugated in four useful verb tenses. I thought they were ready to take on sentence translation.

It was maybe twenty minutes into the assignment when I recognized it had become a cardiac workout for me as I quickly walked from student to student, trying to help each one with questions I hadn't prepared them to answer. But like any green teacher would do, instead of pausing to reevaluate the efficacy of the assignment, I had them keep going.

For a week and a half, I had students working on these translations, and I found myself thinking, *Oh*

Lord, what have I done to these poor children? Not only did I have them doing something I hadn't prepared them for, but I had told them it was worth forty points. That's a lot of points in a high school quarter: It can make two letter grades of difference.

I could see the panic in their eyes.

"Okay, guys," I said calmly, as if I had planned it all to go like this. "So here's the deal. Nobody fails. Everybody gets the full forty points. Okay? So if you could breathe, that would be good."

I grabbed a pencil and a red pen and walked laps around the room. When a student finished a sentence, he would raise his hand, and I would correct it. With the pencil, I would circle any mistakes for him to fix. (Oh, the sighing when they would see me whip out the pencil.) If the sentence was perfect, I would put a checkmark by it in red pen.

"So, I got this sentence wrong?" one student asked.

"No, a red check means 'Hurray, you've done it! It's perfect!'" I said.

"Red checks are bad," she replied. "How about something good, like a star? Could you make it a red star instead?"

We talked for a minute about the knee-jerk reaction we all feel to red pen, and I agreed that a star was an awesome idea. A big *you're-awesome* star.

For days we did this laborious activity. I would star a sentence in red and give the student a cheer to keep going. Some students finally got the hang of translation and finished up in a decent length of time. Some students saw only *fail, fail, fail.*

"No, still not correct," I would say. "Don't give up!"

Toward the end of the Spanish translation torture, I ended up showing a movie while I took stragglers out into the hall, one at a time, to help them finish their sentences.

Mostly, it was awful, and I have tucked that experience into the "stupid beginner teacher ideas" file, which is bulging. But every student got forty points. In fact, some who had been doing poorly brought their grade up significantly, and that made me smile. Every student got forty points, because I decided they were going to, or I would die trying.

At home I thought back through this experience and was moved deeply, as I recognized that I had acted out the very gospel in my classroom.

Isn't God the teacher who gives us the impossible assignment? "You shall be holy, for I am holy" (1 Peter 1:16). Every time I read that verse I think, *Lord, You have got to be kidding.*

But my determination to help my students achieve success was surely the same determination Jesus felt when He headed toward the cross. He was going to make us holy, if He had to die trying.

There is a small bridge that crosses over a creek, just as you come out of our subdivision. Our dear friends live in the same neighborhood, and my son has been grafted in as one of their own sons. One day I crossed the bridge, and my little boy said, "Mom, when Ms. Debby drives over the bridge, I can't feel it." I assume that means she doesn't hit the bridge fast enough to get any lift as she flies over the bumps. A slight difference in driving styles.

I was going over that bridge one day, feeling not only the bumps in the bridge, but the bumps of failure in my heart. My nighttime distress over failures had started creeping into the daytime, and I was starting to see my shame with my waking eyes. But as I flew over the bridge that day, asking God about that yucky feeling about myself, which I was experiencing so often, the Spirit encouraged me that I was thinking so much about my sins and shortcomings because I was growing closer to the Lord.

It's like when you buy your husband a pack of brand new T-shirts, and feel disgusted when you go to lay them in the drawer on top of the old, frayed, sweat-stained shirts. Sometimes the bad looks worst when you see the new right up next to it.

Compared to God's goodness, I was a mess. It was a healthy poverty of spirit I was starting to feel, because I was walking closely with the Holy One.

That moment on the bridge will always be special to me, because God comforted me with the assurance that my growing humility was a sign of how close I was getting to Him. But there was still that miserable feeling, because I imagined the Holy One with a red pen making check marks.

Not stars, but checks.

"You did this wrong, and this wrong, and this wrong."

Red, red, red.

Fail, fail, fail.

"I don't think God intends for you to feel this debilitating misery," my preacher husband said. Still, I struggled with the weight of all I managed to do wrong in a day. Pastor Timothy Keller says that we all know we should be perfect, but every day we know that we aren't.

Sometime later I came across Paul's words to the saints in Ephesians 1:4: "[God] chose us in [Christ] before the foundation of the world, that we should be holy and blameless before him."

That verse became my go-to verse, like my favorite coffee mug: the tall, white porcelain mug that's fluted on the top, the mug I always choose first over any other. I wrapped my mind around the hope of blamelessness, the way my hands wrapped around my hot coffee cup on a cold morning in Montana. For the first time, I began to understand that my becoming flawless was something God decided before He ever breathed life into me. It was something He chose me to be. My blamelessness was His work from the beginning, and He does not fail.

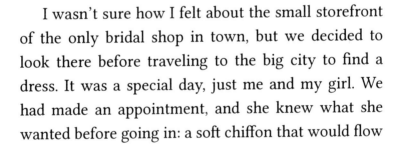

I wasn't sure how I felt about the small storefront of the only bridal shop in town, but we decided to look there before traveling to the big city to find a dress. It was a special day, just me and my girl. We had made an appointment, and she knew what she wanted before going in: a soft chiffon that would flow straight to the floor.

A young woman greeted us, listened to what Jayme had in mind, and then showed her around the modest-sized room lined with dress racks. Jayme walked along, pulling out a dress and then putting it back. The farther she walked, the more I could see the disappointment grow on her face. This was no Kleinfeld's.

We gave each other a look.

It's okay, we'll go shopping in the city, I said to her with my eyes.

But the bridal clerk was really good at her job. She said, "I've pulled a few dresses for you. They're not all necessarily what you had in mind, but come try them on."

I could see my daughter willing me to give up and leave.

"Why not try them on?" I said. "It won't hurt to try them on."

So she tried on a few chiffons, but turned up her nose at them. Then the clerk handed her a stiff taffeta.

Oh brother, I thought. *Was this lady not listening to a word we said? Jayme's going to hate that formal thing.*

After a long time in the dressing room, where I could hear Jayme talking with the store clerk as they got her into that dress, Jayme pulled back the curtain and stepped onto the platform in front of the surrounding mirrors. Oh, I wish you could have seen her face.

This was the dress.

Her hands slowly caressed the fabric over her hips, and she turned to look at herself from all angles.

Hold on, I have to stop writing and cry. Why do those stinkin' kids have to grow up?

On my petite little girl, the dress had to be cinched together a few inches in the back. But it was elegant taffeta with artistic folds. It had a train, but not too much of a train. She didn't even have to think about it: This was the one.

On her wedding day, she looked like a china doll in that dress. I watched her daddy walk her down the aisle, and I watched Dylan's face when he saw her in a thousand dollars' worth of dress and makeup and hair. She looked every bit what a girl hopes to look like on her wedding day: Perfection.

Before God said, "Let there be light. Let there be sky. Let there be animals and birds and trees," He said, "Let her be blameless. Let her come to me in a white, flawless gown."

I was willing to write a big check at the bridal store. We scrimped on other things in the wedding. Friends made cookies and donated decorations. Family members spent hours making table décor by hand. Other friends served in the kitchen and helped us clean up. But when I thought of Jayme's dress, I started to understand the investment Jesus was willing to make in me, and how important it was to Him to see me come to the throne in beautiful white.

⟡

Of the four girls in *Little Women*, I've always related most to Jo. She was loud and bold and was always doing or saying the wrong thing. In chapter 3, Meg and Jo are getting ready to go to a dance at Mrs. Gardiner's house. Meg laments not owning a silk dress, but Jo says poplin is good enough for them.

"Yours is as good as new," says Jo, "but I forgot the burn and the tear in mine. Whatever shall I do? The burn shows badly, and I can't take any out."

"You must sit still all you can, and keep your back out of sight," says Meg.

While desperately trying to hide the back of her outfit at the party, Jo comes upon the neighbor boy, Laurie. He is not ashamed to dance with her, scorched skirt and all.

Somehow, I can't get those dresses out of my mind. Jayme's stunning, flawless wedding dress that fit her like a glove. Jo's scorched old poplin. And you'll forgive me if I imagine Jesus as Laurie: He is going to see the scorched places but put out His hand for you to dance anyway.

He's someone who can take a girl from poplin to silk.

Someone you can talk to when your head hits the pillow.

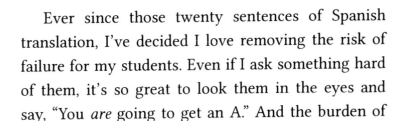

Ever since those twenty sentences of Spanish translation, I've decided I love removing the risk of failure for my students. Even if I ask something hard of them, it's so great to look them in the eyes and say, "You *are* going to get an A." And the burden of that promise rests on me, even though it still requires effort on their part.

This book is about freedom from risk, as we grow in our understanding that the burden of you and me becoming blameless rests on Christ.

With this newfound hope, I try all day long to cooperate with the work Christ is doing in me.

I try.

I set goals. I make sacrifices to do what is right, and I try to actually think before I speak. I serve and give, even when I don't feel like it. I work toward *blameless,* and I find myself succeeding more and more. I'm laying my head down on the pillow at night feeling good about decisions I've made and actions

I've taken during the day. But when I fall short in a day, I lean on the gospel of Christ. He has rescued me from the kingdom of darkness, for a purpose that He will accomplish in His kingdom of light.

Do you know what it's like to wake up in the morning and know you've succeeded before you've even tried? To know God has blamelessness waiting ahead for you, because of your relationship with Jesus? To know, even if you have some setbacks during the day, that God's mercy will be there waiting for you the next day?

This book is about success granted before you try.

And then trying, because *blameless* has always been the plan.

CHAPTER TWO

THE WOMAN WHO DIDN'T WASH HER DISHES

After swearing I would never again live in the heat and humidity of central Texas, I found myself there again, one year into marriage. My husband re-enrolled at our alma mater to get his master's in psychology, and I took up housekeeping in what seemed to me like a luxurious two-bedroom apartment in Temple, Texas.

Shame looks different for everyone, and it comes in degrees of severity, but for me it looked like that kitchen in Texas and my ineptitude at keeping up with the dirty dishes.

Some friends lived nearby, and the wife commented

to me that in order to save money, she never ran her dishwasher. We were very poor college students, so I thought this was sound advice. It was at that point that I started viewing the dishwasher as an evil money sucker. Of course, I didn't even know how much it cost to run a dishwasher, but I assumed it must be a ridiculous amount. So I refused to use it.

That left me washing dishes by hand, except I was too tired to wash dishes, I thought. So I left them for the next day, except then there were so many dishes that I felt overwhelmed. So I left them for the next day. And the next. The kitchen smelled bad. (I hope my mother isn't reading this, because I have never confessed this to her.)

On the weekends, I would groan and set to work doing dishes. I would do dishes for a long time. By hand. Because the dishwasher is of the devil. Then the cycle of failure would start all over again, and I would be too tired at night to do dishes.

The worst day was when I was cooking, and I saw a few cockroaches crawling on the counter. *Had they crawled on the food? I think they crawled on the food.* It was like I had left out an invitation for them, with all those dirty dishes. *Come. Come, little cockroaches and feast. You are welcome here.*

That was a low point, but not low enough for me

to change.

———— ✦✦✦ ————

Maybe your mother is not a children's librarian,
but mine is, so I know a children's book that has to
do with my kitchen habits. In *The Man Who Didn't
Wash His Dishes*, a man lives all alone in his house.
He does his own cooking, but he is too tired at night
to do his dishes. Eventually he runs out of dishes and
starts looking for other items in the house that will
serve as dinner plates, such as the soap dish. He stacks
dirty dishes everywhere, until he can't even find his
own bed. Finally, when everything is dirty and he has
nothing else to eat on, it starts to rain. He takes all of
those dirty dishes outside to get them clean, and, from
then on, he faithfully washes his dishes every night.

Someone should have bought me that book as a
wedding gift.

———— ✦✦✦ ————

One master's degree and two kids later, we were
homeowners for the first time, in my husband's
home town of Kalispell, Montana. We bought a little
yellow house across from a charming old Presbyterian

church, and my young daughter and I used to watch through our front picture window, waiting for brides to come out of the church after weddings. I was a stay-at-home mom with plenty of time to do dishes, except I didn't. King Lemuel's mom taught him that the wife of noble character "looks well to the ways of her household and does not eat the bread of idleness" (Proverbs 31:27). But oh, was I eating that bread.

My mother-in-law lived on seventy-two acres west of town, in a dream house on the side of a mountain. With her husband gone on to heaven ahead of her, she often went south to visit her sister in Tucson. While she was gone, we would go to her beautiful home and enjoy the cable television and stone fireplace.

One time we went out to her place, and we did what we always did: We hung out, ate dinner, and then drove away, leaving the dirty dishes on the counter. "I'll do them next time we come out," I said.

Several days later, our friend from down the street, who was also the youth pastor at our church, knocked on the door of my little yellow house. He said, "Just wondering if it's okay if Pastor Daniel and I head out to your mother-in-law's house to have a planning meeting."

I groaned, as if that were the worst thing he could possibly ask for, and if I remember correctly, I started crying.

He looked at me as if he were sorry he had asked such a horrible favor, and really sorry he had come by at all.

"I left a pile of dirty dishes on the counter," I said.

Of course, to him, my emotional state seemed disproportionate to the small offense of leaving a pile of dirty dishes, but he didn't know that I could not seem to get this area of my life under control. What he couldn't see were the years of piled-up shame.

"It's okay. We can do the dishes," he said.

Louder wailing from me. "You shouldn't have to do the dishes," I said. The poor guy didn't have a chance of saying anything that would make me happy.

A few years ago (two decades into marriage) my husband got frustrated with me.

Matt doesn't get upset with me. When we were first dating, I thought that was the most annoying trait, as if he was practically perfect and I was a mess. (Please don't respond to that.) I would be a jerk, and he would do nothing. "Why can't you just fight with me or something?" I would say. But he was always so nice.

Over the years, I came to appreciate that quality. Despite all the times I felt like a loser when I turned out the lamp at night, it was never because of him. He is a builder-upper. Come to think of it, he probably doesn't feel he needs to tear me down, since I have always done such a good job of that all by myself.

But one day he went into the kitchen and could not find one clean place on the counter. He sighed loudly and said, "Could we at least stack the dishes?" Well, that was a wild and unusual rampage coming from him, and it shamed me.

Why can't I keep up with the dishes? I berated myself.

It doesn't seem hard. A person with even a speck of common sense would say, "Umm, just eat off of the dishes. Wash them. Put them away. The end."

But that's like telling someone, "Just stop smoking." Sometimes change comes slow and hard.

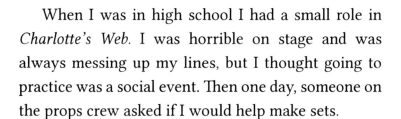

When I was in high school I had a small role in *Charlotte's Web*. I was horrible on stage and was always messing up my lines, but I thought going to practice was a social event. Then one day, someone on the props crew asked if I would help make sets.

"No, thanks," I said.

"You're such a prima donna," she replied.

Now I can confirm that I am, indeed, a prima donna. I always hated doing dishes because they were dirty, and I hate getting my hands dirty. I don't know if that's a character flaw or just something that describes me. I do know that I don't like grease, dried egg, and sticky waffle batter on my hands.

One day in the middle of a Montana winter, my hands were dry and cracking, so I bought rubber gloves to protect them while I was doing the dishes. That was the first step of transformation for me.

Sometimes we have deep-seated issues that explain our real-life messes, and we need therapy for them. I know this, because my husband is a licensed professional counselor. But sometimes we don't need therapy. We just need to spend two dollars on a pair of rubber gloves so the dishes don't feel icky.

At the same time I discovered rubber gloves, I also made peace with my dishwasher. Living the luxurious life, I started spending the money every month to protect my hands. I still didn't know how much it cost to run the dishwasher, but I ran it. *I love you, dishwasher.* Sometimes I even ran the dishwasher when it was not all the way full.

You can gasp and cover your mouth with your

hand, but those lovely clean dishes are worth every penny. And I wonder why I didn't use the dishwasher earlier. Maybe the shame that piled up was partly because I allowed someone else's rule of lifestyle to become my own. Now that's something to think about.

Except for being disgusting, it's probably not that big a deal that I'm lazy at dishes. It's not like I'm out "smoking the marijuana," which we always warned our teenagers against.

But I finally started to see how not doing dishes was compounding problems in other parts of my life. To quote L. M. Montgomery in *Anne of Green Gables,* "All things great are wound up with all things little."

When I would walk into the kitchen at four o'clock in the afternoon, and there was not a clear counter in sight, that meant I had to do dishes for a half an hour before I could even think about starting supper. On many days, I would stand there and say to my family (which must have had a debilitating effect on my children over a long period of time) that I was a complete failure at cooking dinner. Then I would make some mournful sound, throw on my coat, and head to the Wendy's down the street, where we have fully supported the salary of at least one evening shift manager.

The problem began with the mess, and went on to affect mealtimes, but it wasn't just about me making dinner. When you bring home dinner in a paper wrapper, what inspiration is there to set the table and come together as a family? It seems that burgers and pizza should be eaten in the living room, watching television. So to conquer dishwashing was to do something big for my family. Dishes had something to do with nutrition and money and relationships and a peaceful home. The habit mattered.

Buying rubber gloves was a good start, but I've also set a goal to keep the kitchen bar clean. Not the whole kitchen all the time, because come on, but at least the bar where so much activity needs to happen. That seems do-able.

If you'll notice, I'm talking in present tense, which means this is a work in progress.

I have set out to be militant about cleaning the kitchen bar, and I appreciate that Matt has pitched in to help me keep it clean. It helps a lot if at four o'clock, when it's time to think about dinner, I have a clean place to put a cookbook. And someplace where I can put a mixing bowl and some butter. (All good meals start with butter.)

Sometimes I even start cleaning the bar and accidently keep going until the whole kitchen is clean.

<hr />

While I was working on this chapter, I stopped to pull my son's laundry out of the dryer. As I hung up shirts, I thought about everything I've been telling you, and decided that I am crazy. *Why am I writing about cockroaches when I know my mother is going to read this?* I asked myself. *And my daughter and my friends?*

Because this is shame, and we all have it. Maybe you're incredi-woman at doing dishes. I know some of you get up from the dinner table and immediately wash the dishes, and you are my inspiration.

But if it's not dishes, I know you have your own corner of shame. Maybe it's the way you treat people or keeping up with laundry, your temper or what you eat. Maybe it's the bad relationship choices you keep making, or the debt you've gotten yourself into. Shame is that thing you would not want to write into a book chapter and sell to the public.

There is hope for all of us, though, because right now my kitchen is sparkly, and it was sparkly yesterday, too. Sometimes I remember back to when I would let dishes go a whole week, and I don't do that anymore. In fact, I'm starting to get in the habit of actually washing dishes ON THE DAY THEY GET DIRTY. Stop the train.

Last night, I had ten guests for dinner, and when they left, I went straight to the kitchen. I filled the dishwasher, stacked the dishes that wouldn't quite fit, and washed the dishes that needed to be washed by hand. I didn't forget to wipe off the kitchen bar.

When I went to bed, I felt good. I wasn't going to wake up to a mound of dishes, and I wouldn't have to wait for it to rain so I could take all my dishes outside to be washed. I knew that when dinnertime came around the next day, I would walk into a clean working environment where it would be enjoyable to make good food for my family.

It has taken over twenty years for me to stop eating the bread of idleness in the kitchen, but to see that transformation is to see proof that God is alive and working in my life. I've been talking to Him about this weak area for so long, begging Him to help me be more self-disciplined, and He has been helping me change.

So go ahead. Stop in for a visit and come sit down at the bar for a cup of coffee. It's cleaner than it used to be.

CHAPTER THREE

WHAT'S FOR DINNER?

Whitefish, Montana was voted one of the best towns in America in which to enjoy the fall colors. In October, six other writers and I came together from around the country for a three-day blogging retreat. As a result, I found myself in an actual mansion built on the edge of a ski slope looking down over the town of Whitefish, and it *was* a beautiful view.

The mansion had a ski equipment room, with French doors that opened right underneath the chair lift. There were ten bathrooms, including his-and-hers connected to the home theater. Each suite of rooms had its own laundry room that was probably bigger than your kitchen at home, and each suite had its own kitchenette. On each end of the house was a winding grand staircase that led to any of the three levels, and everything was finely finished hardwood and lodgepole pine.

Most exciting of all were the light switches. You could choose whether you wanted full lighting or ambient lighting. I was so sad when I got home and the switch gave me only the option of "off" or "on." (This is how poor people live.)

The main kitchen had a bar that seated at least eight. It also had its own hot water spigot for the built-in pasta pot. In the attached dining room was a small table that seated eight, and under a chandelier was a magnificent round wood table that seated twelve.

In the evening, when the sun was just setting over the orange and yellow leaves of the aspens visible through the picture windows, we gathered for dinner at the round table. There we enjoyed a most comforting *cassoulet* from Shauna Niequist's book, *Bread and Wine: A Love Letter to Life around the Table, with Recipes.* Two sisters had come along to cook for us, and it was a book they couldn't stop raving about. In fact, most of our food during the retreat came from recipes in *Bread and Wine.*

I chatted with the sisters over breakfast in the mornings, and they were delightful women who enjoyed talking about books and who made good coffee, and so I loved them. Also, they both had the cutest short hair, which I envied. They could not have known how weary and failing my heart had been in the kitchen over the years, or how their talk of that book and their comforting food would be used by God to further free my soul from kitchen shame.

When you sit around a dinner table with a bunch of professional writers and two adorable sisters, you should wear Depends, because these are women who know how to tell a story. They are professionals at grabbing audiences, and you feel like you should have paid extra for the entertainment.

Four times, Ruth made Kelly tell her story about accidentally getting her brother pinned down by cops. Every time, it was like we had never heard it before, and we laughed until we were breathless.

In a quiet pause, I said something about the food, and then I don't know how it happened. Probably I was joking, but before long I was confessing to this group that I had felt like a failure in the kitchen for... ever. And I was telling them how I was greeted by name at the Wendy's down the street. And how I cried almost every day because I hadn't made dinner, and what a horrible wife and mother I was.

"I was your neighbor and friend for all those years, and I never knew you struggled with cooking," Tricia said.

I just kept spilling my guts, because these ladies cared. I got to talking about my daughter wanting to eat healthily and how I had determined to make her good lunches, like walnut and rice salad with cranberries sautéed in vinegar, homemade sushi, or enough homemade pita bread for everyone at her table in the high school cafeteria to enjoy.

"Wait, so you know how to cook?" asked one of the ladies.

"Well, yeah. I'm a good cook," I said.

It was a moment of change. I spoke something true that I had not thought about for a long time: I am a good cook.

The next day, I was walking down one of the massive spiraling staircases, and one of the writers came down behind me. She mentioned my feelings of failure at cooking, and I was ready to receive her sympathy.

"What you need is a kick in the pants," she said.

Oh.

My first kitchen failure came on day two of my marriage. I thought I was a good cook, but with that second dinner, I had made all the entrees I knew how to make.

On day three, I cried all day. Hopefully there would be fifty years of marriage, but I did the math, and fifty times 365 days a year equaled 18,250 meals. So the experimenting began.

On the fourth day, I placed a tuna concoction from the *Betty Crocker Cookbook* in front of my husband, who had labored eight hours in the oil field with my dad. We took one bite and looked at each other.

"Arby's?" I asked.

"I think maybe so," he replied.

Foreshadowing.

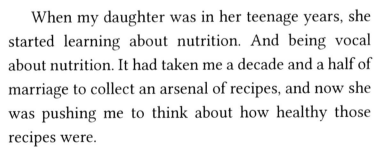

When my daughter was in her teenage years, she started learning about nutrition. And being vocal about nutrition. It had taken me a decade and a half of marriage to collect an arsenal of recipes, and now she was pushing me to think about how healthy those recipes were.

That girl is just like me, and once she learns something, she wants to apply it immediately. All of a sudden, she wasn't happy with white rolls from the bakery. At one point, she even claimed she no longer believed in juice. She apologizes to me about those days, but they were valuable. I started looking at nutrition labels for the first time, and searching for foods that had less pharmaceutical-sounding ingredients.

My son lamented when our bread started to have "stuff" in it: seeds and flax and things.

One night at dinner, I served broccoli, and our daughter taught us how pieces of broccoli were scrubbers for your insides, and corn kernels were sweepers.

We laugh about it now, but that season set me back to where I was in my first week of marriage. Once again, I didn't know what to cook and felt anxious about it. I was trying to please the boys, who thought white bread with enriched flour was from heaven, and the healthy girl who wanted quinoa, dried mangos without added sugar, and natural peanut butter. Added to that was my own desire to be a healthy person, and of course I wanted to provide the best food for my family.

Somewhere in those years, I started to be afraid.

I was afraid to cook anything. Afraid the boys wouldn't be happy. Afraid the girl wouldn't be happy.

Afraid I was poisoning my family with food toxins.

In the late afternoon, I would stand in the middle of the kitchen, paralyzed, unable to breathe, and feeling like I couldn't cook. I started saying out loud, "I am a failure." This became my nightly mantra: "I am a failure in the kitchen."

Ironically, we ended up eating out more because now that I cared more about eating healthily, I couldn't manage to cook anything. We all got sick of pizza and burgers, and I don't know that any of us were happy at mealtimes.

The six foot one inch teenaged boy in our family, the one with the hollow legs, brought out the cat o' nine tails every day at about four thirty.

"Mom, what's for supper tonight?" he would ask.

Hear the swing of the leather, and see the claws pulling flesh from my back?

"I don't know," I would answer. *Because I am a failure in the kitchen.*

"You should write a book about your funny kitchen

stories," my friend said. I don't know if that was because I had tried to chill a salad in the freezer after it got too warm in the car during church. Or if it was because I had taken a pizza out of the oven and promptly turned it upside down in the crack between the oven and the oven door. (Burgers it is. See the theme?) Or if it was because I served chicken tetrazzini to guests, and the next day discovered the chicken in the fridge.

I might lean toward the flaky side, and I might have a deficit in my ability to pay attention to details, but I have a good sense of humor, so I tell these funny kitchen stories on myself all the time.

But I didn't realize that those stories were cementing the "I'm a failure in the kitchen" mantra I had created. In John 10:10, Jesus tells us, "The thief comes only to steal and kill and destroy." I believe the thief was trying to destroy me, by lying about my ability to provide meals for my family. He kept pushing me down in my mind, but Jesus had plans for me to rise.

The two sisters with the adorable short hair had a copy of Shauna Niequist's book, *Bread and Wine,*

which I kept eyeing during the entire retreat. Two months later, it was Christmas break, and I was looking for a book to read for relaxation. I went to my Goodreads page, which is to a librarian's daughter what a bar is to an alcoholic, and there on my want-to-read shelf, I found *Bread and Wine*. When I went to Amazon, it was on sale for $1.99 for Kindle, and with one click, I was reading it.

Shauna's book is a story about gathering people around the table because it makes a difference. It's about enjoying rich food and eating healthily. It has recipes with every chapter, and as I read, I could taste those very recipes because they had been served to us at the retreat: the hearty *cassoulet* and the goat cheese biscuits that made me want to weep with joy.

Shauna talks a lot about what shame does to you, and as I read her stories, I could feel the Holy Spirit next to me. *No more shame in the kitchen*, He said.

I was King Théoden who had listened to Wormtongue until I was only a shell of a woman. And I hope Shauna won't mind me calling her Gandalf the White for releasing me from the poisonous spell of lies.

When I read that book, I woke up to life. *I like to cook*, I said to myself. *I'm a good cook.*

I said it out loud: "I'M A GOOD COOK, AND I

LIKE TO BE IN THE KITCHEN!"

"I wonder what other lies I'm living with that I don't even recognize," I said to my husband while he worked on a puzzle. I was starting to feel like a new woman.

I talked to my daughter, and I told her my cooking journey. She apologized again for making such a big deal about eating healthily when she was younger. But that was part of her journey regarding food, and her prodding me during that time was a part of my journey. Nutrition is important.

"But Jayme," I said. "I think our culture is sick. We've become so consumed with the nutritional value of food that we can't even sit down and enjoy eating anything."

In her book, Shauna Niequist tells about taking a culinary class. She told me (because I know she wrote this book just for my soul) that the chefs walked around saying the same three things over and over: "More heat! More salt! More butter!"

I asked my daughter, who is a gifted artist, if she would paint a mural on my kitchen wall as my birthday gift that year. I told her I wanted it to say something about adding heat and salt and butter. She started sketching immediately.

I've figured out that it's good to read the bread label, but it's also good to melt a half cup of butter into the bottom of a casserole dish and pile French onion soup, rice, broccoli, chicken, and cheese on top of it – and invite someone over to enjoy it and laugh around your table.

Before Jayme finished winter break and left for college, I spent an entire afternoon in the kitchen making food for her and her husband to take with them, and I enjoyed making it. The *cassoulet* from my own kitchen smelled good, and it made her smile. It was a gift to us: the beginning of a blameless and happy kitchen story for a mom and a daughter.

I felt like a failure and had no hope in the kitchen, but God orchestrated a mansion and a luxurious kitchen and a round table. He brought one author, who wasn't even invited to the writer's retreat, to join us at the table, and her food filled my senses before her words ever spoke to my heart. And do you see how those two cute sisters' cooking was part of God's plan to rescue me from failure?

My success was always his objective.

After a long and restful Christmas break, it was time to head back to my Spanish classroom, in an old building that used to be a nursing home. There is one electrical outlet in the whole room, and sometimes I think it smells like old nursing home. Even in the middle of winter, I open the windows to get fresh air.

But despite the tiny size and the age of the place, I love my location. Across the hall is a motherly English teacher who keeps me going with her hugs and greetings at the end of the day. "We did it again!" she says.

And just a few doors down resides the art teacher, a rare treasure tucked into a small private school in northern Montana. She has been known in the big-city world of advertising for her skill, and could definitely use her art in a more prestigious location. Instead she has rows of old bulletin boards all the way down my hall that she keeps filled with the glorious art of K-12 students. Whenever I feel like my room is cramped, I think, *But would I want to leave the gallery in my hall to have a bigger room?*

It was my first day back, and the artist was at the

bulletin board right next to my door, stapler in hand. She was hanging pictures made by young hands and explaining the art to a passerby. "Do you know many of these students don't even know how to set a table?" she asked.

I poked my head out to see the new artwork, and was surprised to see place settings. The students had made artistic pictures of a plate, cup, silverware, and napkin – all in the proper location for a dinner table.

"These kids aren't even eating at a table anymore," the teacher said. "It's a shame that young families aren't sitting down to a nice meal and sharing time together."

It had been two years since I had set a regular dinner table. When my daughter left for college, I couldn't bear the sight of her empty chair, so the menfolk and I took our plates into the living room in front of the television.

But for the grade school children and me, it was time to learn to set the table and have a nice meal again. I went home that day and made dinner. I dusted off the table. With a reverent touch, the Holy Spirit there watching, I gently laid placemats at three chairs. I chose plates and put them just so, with napkin folded to the left, and fork, knife and spoon put on each side.

This was a holy moment. God had removed a lie

from inside my soul and was bringing life to me in the kitchen. It was a service of joy and of freedom, putting food on the table again.

I went to visit my mom in Wyoming, and she sat in the living room with her new iPad. (She is so cool now.) When she came across a recipe for breaded pork chops, she said, "This looks good."

The next morning, I saw that she had written out the recipe and put it on the counter. (Isn't that cute how she wrote it on paper?) In the afternoon, while she was at work, I went to the store and bought pork chops, Italian bread crumbs, and an exorbitantly expensive wedge of parmesan cheese. (If you have not shopped at a store in a town of seven thousand in central Wyoming, you do not know how good the shopping in your town is.)

I went back to Mom's house and grated the fresh parmesan. (I mostly didn't eat it off the plate.) I dipped the pork chops in oil, dredged them in the bread mixture and put them in the oven. When Mom got home, the house smelled so good, we ate immediately. Those pork chops were delicious, and I made them.

I'm a good cook, and I like creating dinner in the

kitchen. That's the truth.

So I ask you: What lies have kept you bound in shame for years? Will you ask God to show you the truth?

CHAPTER FOUR

ON CLEANLINESS AND GODLINESS

A family in our church was hosting a luncheon in honor of a visiting minister from India, and along with the other pastoral staff and a few key families, we were invited to their home. My friends served chai tea, along with a variety of homemade dishes that included elk stew, because we live in Montana. Formal introductions were made, and I felt awkward and humbled to meet someone who was doing such great work for the kingdom of God.

It was after the introductions that I looked down and noticed my friend's coffee table. Magazines were scattered across it, along with a board game and a dirty cereal bowl with a spoon in it. Here I confess to you that I spent more time that afternoon thinking about that cereal bowl than I did about the lost souls of India.

At first I was embarrassed for my friend. How could she not straighten the coffee table before welcoming a houseful of company? Then I remembered that we have dirty cereal bowls lying around our house more days than not. Sometimes they sit there long enough that you have to gently tug on the spoon to get it to come away from the dried milk.

Next I realized that the messy coffee table had no impact on the value of our gathering. The love and greetings were warm in the house that day. We laughed with the Indian emissary about elk stew and how maybe it could be a new commodity in India. We heard stories about God's great work in the sea of lost Indian souls. And the cereal bowl just sat there.

If I could write note to my friend today, I'd say:

Thank you for opening your home to us when it was not stunningly perfect. Thank you for putting more energy into how you greeted me with an affectionate hug than you spent worrying about the condition of your coffee table. Thank you for letting me see that a house can be clean and inviting, but not every inch of it pristine.

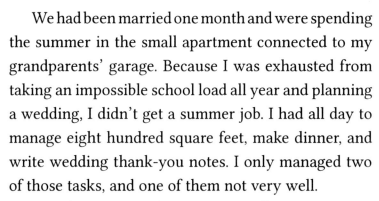

We had been married one month and were spending the summer in the small apartment connected to my grandparents' garage. Because I was exhausted from taking an impossible school load all year and planning a wedding, I didn't get a summer job. I had all day to manage eight hundred square feet, make dinner, and write wedding thank-you notes. I only managed two of those tasks, and one of them not very well.

One day, my grandma unexpectedly came over to bring me something, and I was horrified to open the door and have her see the condition of the apartment. When she looked inside, a flash of shock went across her eyes, but she quickly masked her expression, kindly delivered what she had brought, and left.

That was the first time I felt the sting of my lack of self-discipline in housekeeping. My shame had me shooing Grandma away instead of inviting her in for a visit.

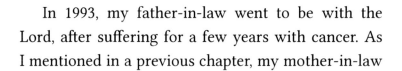

In 1993, my father-in-law went to be with the Lord, after suffering for a few years with cancer. As I mentioned in a previous chapter, my mother-in-law was left alone in a huge log home on seventy-two acres of Montana mountainside.

The next year, I gave birth to our firstborn little girl in a Texas hospital. Matt graduated six months later with his master's in psychology. We were living in poverty after all that schooling, and my mother-in-law was lonely. So we moved north and made her spacious basement our home. It was there God would teach me an important lesson about housekeeping.

The Bible doesn't detail any rules about keeping house, except that we should do it and put elbow grease into it. In Proverbs 31:27, we read that a noble wife "looks well to the ways of her household." But who decides what "well" means? How do we define shame in housekeeping? As I write this, I now understand that we learn a standard of housekeeping from the women in our lives.

My mother's home was always clean and organized. There was a place for everything and everything in its place. It was decorated with care, as Mom changed out decor for each season. From my childhood, I remember regularly cleaning the bathrooms and dusting the interior shutters that hung on the front room windows. Home always seemed perfectly clean to me.

My Grandma Willenbrecht's home was spotless, practical, and perfectly organized. She had some decorations, but they never changed. I remember that before the days of sticky notes, Grandma used her thrift and went to the newspaper to pick up free stacks of colorful paper, the leftover end cuts from publications. She had a dresser downstairs, in which the drawers full of paper were perfectly organized by shapes and colors. Grandma taught me to spend a lot of time keeping the sink clean. She thought a shiny sink was extremely important – maybe because she spent so much time there. She scrubbed it after every use.

My Grandma Eller had a clean and inviting home, although it wasn't organized within an inch of its life. I remember some random stacks of things on a counter or end table. It wasn't to military code like Grandma Willenbrecht's house, but it produced equally good mashed potatoes and just as much laughter around the table. Grandma Eller never said anything to me about the condition of the kitchen sink.

Three very different homes had made up my experience about housekeeping. All three were inviting. They were places where I felt safe and loved.

My best memories were in those living rooms and kitchens and dining rooms. But who was the best housekeeper? Should one receive a reward and the loser duck her head in shame?

When I moved in with my mother-in-law for three years, I added yet another perspective to what it means to look well to one's household. Ask anyone, and they would tell you that my mother-in-law's house is the place to be. She is a Texas lady, and she transported that southern hospitality all the way to Kalispell, Montana. She can whip up dinner for thirty without breaking a sweat. Her large kitchen table always has people around it. Her place is the hub of celebrations, and it is always clean and tidy.

But then I lived with her for weeks and months and a few years. Soon I realized that her house was not immaculate. Especially the kitchen drawers. They were messy, and I wondered how she could live with the randomness of everything in them. In my Grandma Willenbrecht's drawers, all the spoons were facing the same direction, and that perfectionism overflowed into my own ideas of what a kitchen should look like. (Here is where I recognize how much God has helped me grow out of being so judgmental of others, especially in the things that don't matter. That might require a whole new book, though, so I'll move on.)

While my mother-in-law was at work, I did the most horrible thing, and I have since apologized to her several times. Here's one more public apology on record in this book: Sorry, Barb!

I decided to clean out one drawer a day. Without her permission. (*Oh Lord, how did she not send me packing?*) Every day when she got home, I asked her to go through the pile of things from that drawer, to see what she wanted to keep and what she wanted me to donate to the thrift store. *Lord, have mercy.* Do they still do the whole sainthood thing? Because my mother-in-law is at the top of the list.

I thought it was shameful that her drawers weren't tidy.

⟡

When I was young, I read *All-of-A-Kind Family* by Sydney Taylor. In this children's novel, the mother would go into the parlor and hide buttons in obscure places. If the daughters did a good job dusting, they would find all the buttons. That is how I knew that a good woman dusts every millimeter of her home every week. But then there was my mother-in-law with a dust rag in her hand, dusting all the main surfaces, but not "button dusting," as I will call it.

Does God think hitting the high spots is okay?

Before God created me, He intended me to be blameless and holy in His sight. What does that mean when it comes to my role as a housekeeper? Am I living in shame if I don't put away a cereal bowl when company comes, or if I don't dust every inch of every surface on a regular basis? Do my kitchen drawers have to be flawless? I'm learning that part of the journey toward blameless living is defining what *blameless* really means.

Wouldn't it be fascinating to put my mom, Grandma Willenbrecht, Grandma Eller, and my mother-in-law, Barbara, on a panel discussion? I would be the host, and I would present a question to these God-fearing women, all of whom have lived to please the Lord.

"Ladies, how do you think God defines blamelessness, as it pertains to a woman's housekeeping? What do you think He has to say about looking well to one's household?"

Like, if my bathroom sink has crusty toothpaste on it, do I stand in shame before the Lord?

If it has been exactly two months since I've mopped

my kitchen floor, do I need to confess this as sin and failure before God?

If my socks are matched in the drawer ,and organized by color and in order of the last pair worn, does that mean I am considered a holy and blameless housekeeper in God's eyes?

(How can toothpaste on the sink not bother me at all, but a messy sock drawer makes me crazy?)

How can I even know if I am blameless before God, until I know how He defines a worthy housekeeper?

"I think I actually have an obsessive-compulsive disorder," I told my husband one day (the husband who has the master's in psychology). "What do you think?"

He did not respond verbally, but just looked at me. I took that as a bad sign.

One day I was wailing about the condition of the house, so he said he was going to help me clean. You will not believe what he did. I could not believe it.

He looked at what was the dirtiest and cleaned it.

Out of order.

He just started in random places, cleaning a few things in each room. When he was done, the house looked amazing. I stared at him as if he had just swooped in with a cape and rescued me from a fall off a skyscraper. "How did you do that?" I asked.

So yes, I have a problem. It is called obsessive methodology.

I would always start cleaning in the same place and work my way around the house, except I rarely got past the first room, because I had to clean for the buttons, you know. Every surface – seen and hidden – had to be spotless. I took Q-tips to the small places. So I regularly cleaned one percent of my home within an inch of its life, and still it was a mess.

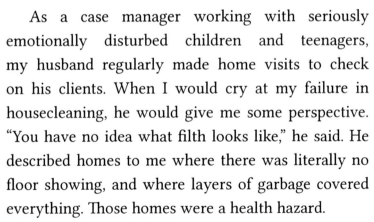

As a case manager working with seriously emotionally disturbed children and teenagers, my husband regularly made home visits to check on his clients. When I would cry at my failure in housecleaning, he would give me some perspective. "You have no idea what filth looks like," he said. He described homes to me where there was literally no floor showing, and where layers of garbage covered everything. Those homes were a health hazard.

There is one simple instruction given by Paul to women, in regard to housekeeping. In Titus 2:4-5, he says that young women should be busy at home.

Busy. That's on the open-ended side of instruction.

Busy making sure everyone has clean underwear and clean surfaces to eat from. Busy making sure her house doesn't become a biohazard that would bring the health department down on her head. Busy cleaning the sink, mopping the floor, and chiseling toothpaste off the sink. How often? God doesn't say.

But obsessive cleaning is not required in order to please the Lord, or He would have specified this, don't ya think? Instead He talks about relationships all the time. He talks about forgiveness, love, and mercy, hospitality and helping the poor. Is my house a welcoming environment that speaks grace and comfort when people walk in? Because it's the people Jesus cares about.

Yesterday my daughter and son-in-law came to visit.

I ran the vacuum in the living room and emptied the garbage. I wiped off the bar in the kitchen and piled the dishes in the sink. My house was warm and cozy, but it was not perfectly clean. The kids and I ate dinner together and watched a movie.

And I went to bed with a smile.

I think there is a shame about our housekeeping that is well-founded. If our families are living in filth, and guests are grossed-out instead of feeling welcome, then I believe God wants us to grow in being busy and doing a better job cleaning. But I think there is also a shame about housekeeping that simply comes from standards we have established that aren't necessarily what God had in mind.

Maybe you had a mom who was obsessive about the house being spotless and you feel you have to live up to that. Or maybe you've read magazine articles or blog posts that give extensive cleaning schedules, and you feel like you have to follow all those steps, or be a complete failure as a woman. Or maybe you have a neat-freak friend whose house always looks pristine, and you measure yourself next to her standard. From somewhere, you have developed a perspective on caring for your home.

But you know, it's our souls God intends to make spotless, not our kitchen drawers or our linen closets. When we wake up and do housework, we need to please *Him*. Good news, sister. His housekeeping standard is do-able. He wants us to be busy at home and to look well to the ways of our household. What if you get up in the morning and look around at what most needs done in the house today –and you just get busy doing it?

Maybe you're much closer to making the Lord smile than you thought you were.

CHAPTER FIVE

A Body That Won't Stop

Lying flat on my back in the dentist's chair, I fielded questions from the hygienist who was sitting at the computer behind me.

"Do you brush your teeth at least twice a day?" she asked.

"Yes," I said. (*I am awesome*, I thought.)

"What kind of toothbrush do you use?" she asked.

"Sonicare," I said.

"That's the very best," she said. (*Don't you know it, sister!*)

"Do you floss?" she asked.

"Yes." (Fist bump.)

"How many times a day?"

"Twice," I said. (*Let the confetti fly, hygiene lady.*)

All the way through my cleaning, the hygienist told me how great my hygiene was, and how perfectly I had cared for the back molar that was brought to my attention at the last cleaning. I rocked the whole exam. No cavities.

I was bragging shamelessly about this to my son on our way to the mall. I told him that when I used to go to the dentist, several years ago, the hygienist would ask if I flossed.

"No," I would say.

"You need to floss every day," she would say.

"I know," I would say, hanging my head just like Tom Dooley in the song.

I told my son how I got sick of the shame of not flossing, so after one embarrassing dental visit, I decided I was going to floss for thirty days in a row until it became a habit.

"How did you remember to keep flossing for thirty days in a row?" he asked.

"Well, because I decided I was going to. I just decided to do it or else," I said. At the time I didn't have words to explain to him how desperate I was to never be ashamed in the dental chair again. And God had given me hope that if I would just roll up my sleeves and put in some effort, combined with His power at work in me, I could change.

That is how I became the best patient ever to walk into the Montana Center for Laser Dentistry. Probably they will hang a plaque with my name on it.

A plaque. Get it?

I met my man in Texas in 1988. I was a sophomore at the University of Mary Hardin-Baylor, and he was a freshman. I weighed 115 pounds at 5 foot four. He weighed 115 pounds at six foot one. To say the least, he was self-conscious about how skinny his legs were.

We got married in 1991, and I remember the day he celebrated weighing 140 pounds. He was simply beefy at that weight. Or a beefcake. Something like that.

Then he hit his thirties and finally caught up with his metabolism. He sat on the edge of the bed in shock one day, wondering how he had gotten to a place where his stomach was hanging over his belt. I saw a steely glint come into his eye, and he set his jaw, like his favorite Louis L'Amour character would do.

"I'm doing a boot camp," he said.

We paid the fees to The Summit fitness center, and

Matt set his alarm clock for five o'clock a.m. Every day he would get up, put on his workout clothes, and grab his truck keys.

"Should I drive you there?" I would ask. His eyes didn't appear to be open yet, and I thought that might be an important element in driving oneself to the gym.

Matt did this routine for thirty days in a row. Around six thirty, I would hear the garage door open, and he would stumble through the door and go straight back to bed. I was always amazed that they allowed him to operate motorized workout equipment in that condition.

Soon, I could see the pounds begin to drop off him. Then he asked for new pants with a smaller waistline, which we had not budgeted into his workout routine. He started to look good. (Say that with four Os.) I started to hug him a little longer and reach for his biceps a little more. Biceps of steel.

You cannot see it, but I just had to stop and collect myself.

We had a marital summit meeting in our thirties, where that man and I discussed what kind of older people we were going to be.

I was doing medical transcription, which meant I was typing all the information from people's doctor visits every day. I could hear how people's weight, deconditioning, and bad habits were affecting their physical and mental health. I was typing about diseases and injuries that ultimately were the result of being unfit.

Matt and I talked about what kind of servants we wanted to be for the Lord in the years to come. We made a decision: *We are going to be healthy older people, Lord willing.* At least as much as it was in our power to control.

As I write this, we've both had a horribly sedentary year, mostly because grief and other trials have hit our household, and it has been one of the hardest years of our lives together. But we're both coming up for air again and have been warming up the treadmill.

Because we want to be strong and fit, we keep trying.

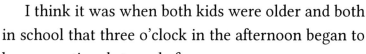

I think it was when both kids were older and both in school that three o'clock in the afternoon began to be an emotional struggle for me.

I love having time alone. Give me hours by myself,

to work to my heart's content and to be creative. But at three o'clock in the afternoon, I kept finding myself in the kitchen on an insatiable snacking binge. I could eat healthily all day, but at three, I stopped caring and began reaching for cookies and milk – and maybe a few more cookies. And maybe one more.

One day, I stopped before snacking and ran a diagnosis. *Why am I eating like this at the same time every day?*

I was eating because I was lonely. Seven hours by myself was wonderful, but in that seventh hour, an emotional switch was flipped. I needed people. I needed someone to talk to and someone to care about what I had done during the day. I needed a hug.

My soul was hungry.

I was reaching for food, but there weren't enough cookies to satisfy.

I took action. First, I knew that I didn't have anything good to grab for a snack. I thought about what food I could eat, and there I encountered another small battle. It felt selfish to spend money to buy myself the more expensive healthy snacks. I think this is a mom thing when finances are limited. We spend money on the family first, and not on ourselves. But I decided it was time to take care of myself.

Mom had given me the cutest glass canisters that

she found at the thrift store for fifty cents each, so I lined those up on the counter, out in the open, and filled them with good things to eat. I bought pistachios and peanuts. I got Triscuits and some individual cheeses made by laughing cows. I also bought some granola bars, cottage cheese, and applesauce. Everywhere I turned in the kitchen, I could quickly put my hand on something decent for an afternoon snack.

Next, I started paying attention to the loneliness that would come at three o'clock. I called it loneliness, because putting a truthful name to a problem is a good first step to change. So when the clock turned to three – and it was almost the exact same time every day – I started talking to the Lord while I cracked open pistachios.

Sometimes I forget God is a real-life companion. He is someone to talk to. Someone who replies and who can fill the heart. From the psalmist we hear this plea: "Satisfy us in the morning with your steadfast love, that we may rejoice and be glad all our days" (Psalm 90:14). I began to pray, "Satisfy me, in the middle of the afternoon, with your steadfast love."

Three o'clock was transformed from a time of shameful binge eating, to a reasonable time for a snack I could be proud of, and a filling and intimate encounter with God.

You have to know what you're really hungry for.

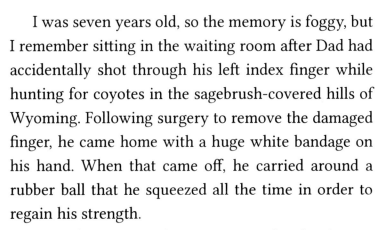

I was seven years old, so the memory is foggy, but I remember sitting in the waiting room after Dad had accidentally shot through his left index finger while hunting for coyotes in the sagebrush-covered hills of Wyoming. Following surgery to remove the damaged finger, he came home with a huge white bandage on his hand. When that came off, he carried around a rubber ball that he squeezed all the time in order to regain his strength.

But what I remember most was the day he got upset when he grabbed his normal stack of Oreos and milk. With phantom feeling in his finger, he thought he was holding onto the top of the stack. He wasn't, and all the Oreos fell to the floor. That's when Dad realized he wasn't going to be able to hold as many cookies as he used to, and I remember thinking it was a great tragedy.

Cookies were a big deal at our house. Mom had a pottery bowl that took two arms to lift, and we had an agreement that I would make the cookies in that bowl, if she would do the dishes. (As you can tell by the previous chapter, dishes weren't my shining gift, even when I was younger.)

I made cookies with two cups of Crisco. It was a long time before I would think about whether that was the most heart-healthy recipe or not. I just knew those cookies were our favorites, and I made them often. I don't remember there being a limit on how many cookies we could eat. Stacks of Oreos and stacks of homemade chocolate chip cooks were normal, and I ate them after school and after dinner.

Mom stayed at home when we were growing up, and I remember getting off the bus and coming into the house, to find her spooning out cookie dough from the pottery bowl. Hot cookies waited for us a lot, and I give her Best Mom Ever for this gift to us. It was a tradition I kept with my own kids, just to see their faces when they would walk in and sniff the fragrance of freshly-baked cookies.

But then one fine day in my mid-thirties, I couldn't snap the jeans that had always fit before, and I knew the cookie habit had to change. I grew up always eating something sweet after dinner, and I wasn't ready to give that up. But maybe I didn't need a whole stack of something sweet? So one night I ate two cookies instead of three.

I'll wait a second while you stand in awe at the level of control I was able to exert over myself.

For quite a long time, I forced myself to only eat two cookies. Then I did something tricksy. I started making smaller cookies.

I know. You probably would have tried to talk me down from such a drastic life change, but sometimes you have to go big.

Instead of heaping the spoon with dough hanging over the edge, I just filled the spoon with a mound of dough. And then I still only allowed myself two cookies.

That's right.

After that, sometimes I would be ridiculous and only allow myself one cookie. And I found a cookie recipe that called for butter instead of Crisco, so it's healthy. (Shhh.)

I got used to eating a much smaller desert, and now I can't eat a big one. It tastes too sweet and feels too indulgent.

I don't know if there should be a whole section in a book about how someone tried to eat fewer cookies after dinner, but for me it was a big habit change toward being a healthy woman.

One day I watched a talk show, and they hosted

a guest nutritionist who talked about where to put things in your refrigerator so that you would be encouraged to eat the better foods.

Sometimes knowledge is all you need for a big change.

As soon as the nutritionist was done talking, I went and spent an hour rearranging my fridge.

I've done a lot of crazy things in my life, because I tend to hear good ideas and try to implement them immediately. My family hated my Amish novel phase, in which I announced that we were now going to be the big family that cooked and cleaned house together. That one didn't stick so well. But the fridge arrangement has been a lasting change.

The lady on TV said that vegetable bins are where healthy foods go to die. She was right. I would buy fruits and vegetables at the grocery store every week, because I was going to be the perfectly healthy eater. At the end of the week, I would throw those slimy foods away and buy some more.

During the time of this TV show, a Panda Express had opened up in our town. Have you seen their refrigerator? They have a clear glass fridge in their kitchen that you can see from where you order, and inside are stacks of clear plastic bins filled with prepared vegetables.

Red peppers. Carrots. Broccoli.

They're so beautiful, you almost want to eat them.

So in my fridge renovation I put the least healthy foods down in the vegetable bins. Down went the sour cream and grape jelly. Down went the condiments.

I had a really cool basket a friend brought back for me from her trip to Africa, so I bought some lovely fruit and placed it in the basket. This went on the top shelf of the fridge.

I washed lettuce and put it in one clear plastic container. It made the second shelf. I prepared carrot sticks and put them in another clear plastic container. What do you think of that, Panda Express?

Presentation of food is a powerful force. When I would open the fridge and see the pears and apples in the African basket, I would want to eat some. And I would see the carrot sticks and put some on my lunch plate.

Thank you, nutrition lady.

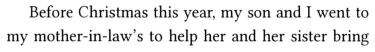

Before Christmas this year, my son and I went to my mother-in-law's to help her and her sister bring up their Christmas decorations from the crawlspace.

We brought it up, and brought it up, and brought

it up.

"We're going to get rid of some of this," they said. I teased them about how many decorations they had, as I filled their guest room with boxes, but I figured it wasn't all that much for a lifetime of collecting. When we were done, I had worked up a sweat, but it was so rewarding to be able to help them. It felt good that I was strong enough to lift and carry all those boxes.

The writer of Proverbs says a wife of noble character "dresses herself with strength and makes her arms strong" (Proverbs 31:17). Now that I'm in my mid-forties, I've given up the dream of returning to my twenty-year-old waistline, and I'm starting to get an extra chin.

But I can maintain strong arms.

In his letter to the Ephesian church, Paul gives us hope that God has always intended His people to be blameless. Farther along in the letter, Paul writes, "For we are his workmanship, created in Christ Jesus for good works, which God prepared beforehand, that we should walk in them" (Ephesians 2:10). God has prepared good works for us to do, and we need strong arms to do those tasks.

Does God care if I floss, or if I eat fewer cookies than I used to? Does He care if I develop the self-discipline to get on the treadmill, followed with bicep curls and lunges? I know the answer is yes. As I move away from the undisciplined life of eating for comfort and being too sedentary, I move toward a life of high-energy service in God's kingdom.

What we really want to feel good about, at the end of the day, is that our arms have been strong for the tasks God has given us. We eat well and exercise enough to have a healthy vigor for taking care of our homes and family, plus enough energy to love and care for the people God puts in our path.

CHAPTER SIX

So Much Stuff

You can't understand my perspective on shopping unless you've grown up in the heart of Wyoming, in a town hidden away in a valley among the Wind River Mountains.

As teenagers, my friends and I used to "drag" Lander's main street for Friday night entertainment in the summertime. That meant we drove the two-mile length of town. If the lights were in our favor, this grand adventure took three minutes. Then we turned around and drove back in the other direction, honking and waving at friends.

On one end of town was an Alco, which made

a modest attempt to be a K-Mart. On the other end of town was a Pamida, and it was quite an outing if you shopped in both of those stores in one day. In the center block of downtown was a beautiful store called Wildwood, and that was the only place to go if you wanted to get something nice for your mom's birthday. They carried a lot of glass and breakable items, and you always talked a little quieter in there.

It was a three-hour drive from Lander to the closest mall, and if you could see its size, you would think calling it a mall was a joke.

Do you remember the book about the country mouse and the city mouse? Well, we were the country mice. A few times a year, we piled into the car to visit my aunt, the big city mouse. She and her husband managed Brooks Towers, one of the largest high-rise apartment complexes in the center of downtown Denver.

About an hour out of Denver, the traffic would pick up, and Dad would start barking at us to be quiet and sit back. Even from that far away, we would see the city lights and the clump of skyscrapers towards which we were headed. In those days we didn't wear seatbelts, so we would hang over the front seat in our excitement.

All I could think about was shopping.

Aunt Karyn and Uncle Lennie would put us up in the penthouse suites as guests, which was a thrill, but I couldn't wait to take the elevator downstairs and go to the stores that surrounded Brooks Towers. There were more stores in downtown Denver than in all of Wyoming. In addition, almost every trip we made to Denver included a drive to Cinderella City, which was a real mall with escalators.

And so I learned that shopping was entertainment and buying things was happiness.

I don't know why the Lord landed me in central Texas for college – this little Wyoming girl who takes after her father and cannot bear heat. By heat I mean anything over sixty-five degrees and zero humidity. But Texas is where I unloaded my humble dorm supplies from my parent's car, in the sun and humidity of an August day. I had never felt that kind of miserable heat, and soon learned to dress in the lightest cotton clothes I had.

This was ironic, because I grew up with the lecture that "cotton kills." If you wear cotton in a Wyoming winter, you'll die of hypothermia. "Wear wool," Dad always used to say, but he was talking about being caught outside in subzero temperatures and wind chills that make your lungs hurt. What I didn't know was that Texans manufacture their own subzero temperatures by way of air conditioning. So I went to class on my first day, and remembered that "cotton kills." I was going to die in Texas, either by sweltering outside or being frozen in the AC. Could there be no happy medium?

I had very little money, but when it was eighty degrees and eighty percent humidity outside, I went to the mall to buy a cardigan for wearing in the air-conditioned classrooms. It seems strange that this trip to the mall is still so vivid to me, but I remember how I felt when I was shopping for that cardigan. I was painfully homesick, being thrown into a new state, new school, and new culture, with no friends or family nearby. I remember feeling that this shopping trip would make me happy, that a cardigan could do something for the needs of my soul.

I was also aware there was something very wrong in my heart. I felt uncomfortable that I had learned to find satisfaction in "retail therapy." It was the first conversation God had with me about finding satisfaction in Him, instead of in buying new stuff.

I ate hundreds of peanut butter and jelly sandwiches when I was growing up, because I was that picky kid who turned up her nose at everything put on the table. Then one time, I came down with a nasty head cold. I made myself the usual PB&J, but it tasted horrible. My inability to smell ruined the culinary experience, and after taking only a few bites, I threw the sandwich away.

Years later, that yucky PB&J would have a significant impact on my spiritual life.

One day, I read John's words to the followers of Christ: "Do not love the world or the things in the world. If anyone loves the world, the love of the Father is not in him" (1 John 2:15). I had to confess that I loved shopping and getting new things. Every day, I would stand in front of my closet and long for new clothes. I was constantly thinking about how to get new jewelry. I had a growing mental list of things I wished I could add to my home decor. I was preoccupied with plans for getting things I couldn't really afford.

How do we change those driving desires within us? I thought about how much I had loved peanut butter and jelly sandwiches, until one day I hated them because of that head cold, so I turned that experience into a prayer: *Lord, please let clothes and jewelry and house stuff taste like PB&J to a girl with a head cold. Change the flavor of these things in my heart, so I turn up my nose at the mention of them.*

I wanted the things of this world to taste: Flat. Unsatisfying. Disappointing.

After praying that prayer over a long period of time, I found myself in Target looking at the cheerful spring dishes in the housewares section (always a weak spot for me). For a brief moment, my love for pretty dishes was strong. I am easily wooed by color, and I think the Target marketers know this. Salmon. Turquoise. Kumquat. They call to me.

This was when the Lord answered this prayer for the first time, and it's proof that God will help us move toward that blameless life He wants for us.

There I was standing in the aisle, my mouth salivating over colorful plates, when I had my first flat-PB&J feeling, an experience of knowing deep in my heart that the dishes on the shelves had beautiful colors, but offered nothing to satisfy my soul. In that moment, the devil's salesmanship crashed into God's answer to my prayer.

I have a friend who has lost her sense of smell. As a result, most foods have little flavor for her. When other people are raving about the smell and taste of something, she has no reaction. You can pull hot, buttery cinnamon rolls out of the oven, and the smell does not affect her at all. I feel sad for her loss. In the same way, it feels unnatural to me to lose the deep longing to buy things. I feel like I've lost one of my senses.

But in losing my desire to buy things, I am learning what it means to desire God more.

After my father went to be with the Lord last year, my aunt and I were talking about the new drive Mom has to avoid burdening us kids with cleaning out a bunch of stuff from her house when it's her turn to go to heaven.

My aunt had an elderly friend who told her, "We spend the early years of our life accumulating things, and the later years of our life trying to get rid of it all."

My desire for stuff has been diminishing over the years, but with this new reality of the brevity of life, I am feeling even more detached from the acquisition process. I'm thinking, *Why not skip the "getting" stage?*

When my daughter was in first grade, we made the decision to sell our old house, with its crumbling foundation and terrifying electrical wiring, and build a new house in a beautiful new neighborhood northeast of town.

After showing the old house almost every day for months, it finally sold, and we had one week to pack up and move. If you care about your sanity, I do not recommend this. We rented a storage facility and stored our belongings there until we moved into our new home.

A few months later, I was chatting with our pastor. Laughingly, I described how the boxes of my daughter's clothing, from baby clothes to the present, made two stacks that went from floor to ceiling in that storage unit. She was the first grandbaby on both sides of her family, and she was spoiled.

"You're hoarding those clothes," my pastor said to me.

"What?" I said.

"You're hoarding. Why are you keeping all those clothes when you could be sharing them?"

I almost felt like I had been slapped across the face, and at first, I was indignant. But as I thought on my pastor's words all day, I realized he was right: Someone could be using those clothes. Moms get awfully attached to memorabilia connected with their sweet babies, so I still had some internal work to do. But I thought of Jesus' instruction: "Do not lay up for yourselves treasures on earth" (Matthew 6:19).

When we moved our stuff into the new house and were able to reach the back of the storage unit, I asked around and gave those clothes to a mom who had a little girl. Later, she had more girls, and they all wore those clothes that had been my daughter's. For years afterwards, I would see her, and she would tell me how helpful the clothes had been.

⁂

My husband tells people that he knows he had better make himself useful, or he's going to end up at the Salvation Army Thrift Store. (It could be true. Let's not test that theory.)

Years ago, I made a commitment to buy nothing for my home that is not an item of necessity, and I have kept to that. These days, I work hard to get rid of things as well. Of course, I want to have a cozy home, so I have some pretty decorations, but I have been paring them down significantly.

I go through my clothes a few times a year, and keep only what I really wear, plus that one pair of jeans that I still have dreams of snapping one day.

I will not buy jewelry for myself, and I got rid of all but my favorites.

I made a commitment to buy a minimal amount of makeup, which means spending about thirty dollars a year.

And I have learned to enjoy beautiful things without having to own them. When I pass something in the store that catches my attention, I usually say to myself, *That is beautiful, but you don't have to possess it to enjoy its beauty in this moment.*

My refusal to store up treasures for myself has extended to the outside of my home, too. I used to long for beautiful landscaping and lovely outdoor furniture. I don't know how many times I walked by patio sets in Home Depot and had a burning desire to own them. Now I just don't care. God has helped me stop longing for stuff in this world. (Okay, well mostly. I still get pretty excited over a new skirt.)

I wanted to please the Lord, in desiring to store up treasures in heaven more than treasures on earth, but the love for stuff in this world was so strong. I never could have changed those desires by myself, but I can see Him at work, transforming the passions of my heart until I lean toward things of eternal significance.

I don't lie in bed plotting purchases anymore.

That's amazing evidence that God slowly purifies the hearts and minds of His children.

CHAPTER SEVEN

WASTE NOT

Grandma grew up in the Great Depression. I remember her talking about living on potatoes, and I later found out that she suffered physically for the rest of her life because of the malnourishment she experienced in those years.

Grandma knew how to make her pennies go farther than anyone I've ever met. One day we were at Wendy's for lunch, and I watched her pull out her change purse and count out coins to pay for her lunch. "Always spend your change," she said.

I've tried to copy Grandma in this thoughtfulness about every penny, but for the sake of my marriage,

I use dollar bills at the drive-through when I'm with that man of mine. If you could see the grumpy look my husband gave me, those few times I handed him a load of change to pay for our dinner – I stopped doing that, I can tell ya. Wow.

I could talk about Grandma's thrifty lifestyle for pages, but I mostly want you to know about her spatula. When she whipped up cake batter, or mashed potatoes, or anything else, she would use that rubber scraper to get every molecule of food out of the bowl and into the pan or serving dish. Then she would use her finger to get every bit of food off the rubber scraper and into the dish. Grandma did not waste anything.

When I was a teenager, I felt sorry for my friend, because she said her mom would kill her if she didn't save the baggies from her lunch. One day I was at her house, and I saw for myself that her mom had washed the sandwich bags and set them upside down on the windowsill to dry. I thought that lady was crazy.

But the other night I was gone for the evening, hosting a women's event at church. When I got home, I was delighted to see that Matt had cleaned the kitchen. (Bless him!) The dishwasher was loaded, and all the big dishes were washed.

He said, "You should really thank me when you see that I washed those plastic freezer bags and put them in the sink drainer." I can picture him looking at those bags and holding them over the garbage can, in great temptation to throw them out. But no, his is a sacrificial love, the kind Jesus has for the church.

I was just talking to a friend of mine last Saturday. She said she had made a meal on Tuesday that they still had not eaten, and she was going to be embarrassed if she had to throw it away. I told her I would be glad if she did, because it would assuage my guilt for all the food I've thrown away in my life. I don't know how many times I've thawed meat from the freezer, with great plans to make a meal, only to procrastinate so many evenings in a row that finally I had to throw out the raw meat. (See the previous chapter on my years of failure in feeding my

family.)

Something inside me knows it is wrong to waste food, or anything else I possess. I feel shame when I throw away something that could have been used, if I had only been more diligent.

My mother-in-law pulled out her iPad, as we sat at her kitchen bar together. "Let me show you pictures of the quilts we finished while we were at Bena's," she said.

There are three sisters. Barb is my mother-in-law, and she lives with her baby sister, Joan. She and Joan spent several weeks visiting their older sister, Bena, down in Tucson. In Bena's front room, they set up their quilt rack and stretched one of their grandma's quilts out on it.

Their grandma pieced together stacks and stacks of quilt tops and squares in her lifetime. Even when she was elderly and could hardly see, she would get her daughter to thread a row of needles before she went to work. Then she would piece quilts until she ran out of needles.

Their grandma is gone now, and her unfinished quilts have been in storage at Bena's for many years. The sisters have decided to finish quilting all those quilt tops and give them to the girls in the family. We already have ours: a peach and white pattern, on which they put a brown backing. My daughter received her finished quilt recently, as well. To see the hand stitching in these quilts is a treasure.

As we scrolled through pictures of the quilting sessions, Barb pointed out the various fabrics. "Those pieces are cut from the dress I wore in fifth grade," she said.

Aunt Joan added, "And that is part of my first nursing uniform."

Considering the herculean effort required for me to replace a button on an item of clothing, I can't even imagine cutting apart our old clothes and sewing them into quilts by hand. The thought makes me laugh out loud. But I wonder what happened. When did we stop using things until they truly were of no use anymore?

───◇※◇───

I have thought for many years on this topic. Was my shame over wastefulness one of those feelings I was trained to have by a thrifty grandma, a mom who recycled, and a dad who barked at us if we left the water on while we brushed our teeth? Or was this uncomfortable feeling about being wasteful coming from the Spirit of God? My husband wasn't super big on all my conservation ideas (sometimes he comes and turns the water on while I'm brushing my teeth, just to be ornery), so that also made me wonder if I was being ridiculously conservative or if these desires were from the Lord.

I found three passages in the Bible that gave me a sense that the Lord values thrift and conservation. First, in Genesis 1, I read the story of creation, and in Genesis 2:15 it says, "The LORD God took the man and put him in the garden of Eden to work it and keep it." That seems to be a general instruction for all of us. We're on the earth God made, and He intends us to take care of it.

One day, my dad learned that his local landfill was reaching capacity, and they had begun charging people by the weight of what they dumped there. You should have heard the long, impassioned speech he made about how much plastic and cardboard Americans often use to package a tiny item. He thought if we would just lay off the excess packaging, it would make a huge change in landfills. Dad taught me to take care of the world.

Another Bible story that speaks to wastefulness is found in Luke 16:19-21: "There was a rich man who was clothed in purple and fine linen and who feasted sumptuously every day. And at his gate was laid a poor man named Lazarus, covered with sores, who desired to be fed with what fell from the rich man's table." The rich man had so much food that it fell from the table, and he didn't even notice.

My grandma used a rubber spatula because she remembered what it was like to live in poverty. She wasn't going to let any crumb from her table go to waste. She used the extra food to be generous to her family and generous to others. Being careful with food comes from a heart that is mindful of the poor, and caring for the poor is at the core of God's heart.

One day I was reading a *National Geographic* magazine, because I love the stories about people around the world. I remember one gloomy picture of an elderly woman who was sitting at a rough wooden table. In front of her was a tiny pile of rice, and she was rationing it into even smaller piles to last her a week. I will never forget that picture, because I looked at it and thought about her life for a long time. Would she even be eating a spoonful of rice each day?

How can I casually scrape leftover rice into the garbage when I've become aware of hunger in this world? How can I not be careful with food and overflow with thankfulness to God for every bite of it? God has slowly increased my awareness of the poor, and being aware of poverty has changed how I live.

A third verse that influences me toward conservation is Proverbs 14:1: "The wisest of women builds her house, but folly with her own hands tears it down." God has done so much work in my life to teach me to spend money wisely, to care for my home, to make good food for my family, and to decrease our family's personal spending in order to increase our giving to God's kingdom. Wastefulness tears down that work.

Is thrift and conservation of this earth a part of living blamelessly before the Lord? I think so.

I started watching this show called *Hoarders*, and I loved it because these people's homes were such a mess that I instantly felt better about mine. I liked it, too, because it was a show about getting organized, and organizing always makes me happy. But one day, the show was so disturbing I had to turn it off. The homeowners were mentally ill, and the state of their home actually made me gag. I won't tell you the grossest thing they showed, but I will never get it out of my mind. So my thoughts swing from my thrifty grandma to these people who had a compulsion to save everything, to the point that the health department would remove them from their home if something didn't change. Both were saving, but to what end?

Grandma was unbelievably frugal, but she was also one of the most generous people I've ever known. She always took yummy food to church potlucks and to sick shut-ins. I always left her house with something in my hands, like a new dress or a plate of cookies. She brought us a huge bucket of Kentucky Fried Chicken the day my other grandma passed away. In high school, she loaned me one of her cars to drive. She was conservative with her resources so she could be generous to others.

When Grandma went to be with the Lord, we cleaned out her apartment. In one corner was a cardboard bucket that had originally contained ice cream or potato chips or something. For as long as I could remember, she had used that little bucket as a garbage can. I've carried that image as a lesson to me. When I'm tempted to upgrade just so I can have something shiny and new, I ask myself if there's really anything wrong with the old. Could I use it a lot longer and save my money, so I could be generous to someone instead?

The other day, I made a lovely dinner of pork chops, steamed veggies, and a rice and quinoa blend. When I was cleaning up the kitchen that night (thanks to the work of God in my life), I came to the leftovers. There was no meat remaining, because I have Montana men. In a bowl was a large spoonful of rice that normally I would have thrown away. There was steamed cauliflower left, because the boys think it's gross and pick out the broccoli and carrots for themselves. Normally I would have thrown away that little bit of vegetables, too. But I felt the Spirit nudge me not to be wasteful. So I got a plastic container and put the rice in first, and then the cauliflower on top. The next day, I ate those leftovers for lunch, and I thanked God I had so much rice to enjoy for one meal.

There aren't any rules. There's no commandment from the Lord that we must recycle freezer bags. He doesn't tell us that in order to please Him, we must turn off the water while we brush our teeth, or make a quilt out of last year's T-shirts. But He does slowly work in us, until we feel a life-changing compassion for the poor, and a heightened determination to use our own resources well. This is when we find we have pleased Him at the end of the day.

CHAPTER EIGHT

TO THE ANT

Today is a beautiful day in mid-April. There is still a good amount of snow on the peaks behind our house, but the sun is shining, and for the first time in many months, it is warm enough to open the windows and let in some fresh air. There is no school today, so I have buckled down to do some spring cleaning.

Which explains why I have checked Facebook thirty-seven times since I woke up.

Sometimes, I am incredible. I clean bathrooms, do laundry, pay bills, and make dinner. Then there are the times like right now. I am taking a break from twelve minutes of strenuous spring cleaning, so I can write about laziness.

Several years ago we made the decision, as a church, to sell our old building and construct a new one in a different location. I think it was the woodpeckers doing percussion on the back wall of the sanctuary during the morning service that finally sealed that decision. Or maybe it was the annual flooding of the preschool wing during spring thaw. But I remember the day we voted to build. It was so exciting!

Then began the long year of building, and the regular call on Sundays for volunteer labor. It was the worst year ever. There was not one molecule in my body that wanted to work on that church building, but I felt guilt every time they announced the need for volunteers. If I stayed home instead of helping, I felt ashamed.

So one day I was quite heroic. I put on work clothes, arrived at the church and wandered into the would-be sanctuary. There were people crawling all over the church like ants, working in every part of the building. Someone handed me a broom, and I swept up the piles I could see. I finished that job, and didn't know what to do next.

I stood in the sanctuary feeling lost and inept. How did everyone seem to know what to do? With tears of shame pooling in my eyes, I quietly left the church building. On that day, I created a new label for myself. *I am lazy*, I thought. *They are hardworking people, and I am lazy.*

I held the flier for Rock This City in my hand. It was a service project designed by one of the big churches in town, in which everyone was invited to serve somewhere in Kalispell for three hours. Surely I could be a hard worker for three hours. Maybe this was my chance to redeem myself, and show the world that I was not a slacker (because the whole world thought I was).

Opening the flier, I began reading through the different options of service, and my heart sank. I read about projects like painting and weeding and cleaning. Yuck, yuck, yuck. Nothing sounded appealing to me, but I squared my shoulders and steeled myself to work somewhere.

Then I came to the last page, and there was one choice that made me lean forward. They were asking people to go spend three hours with the residents of a nursing home. I had always loved going to the nursing home, especially at Christmas when we would walk through the halls and sing Christmas carols. Now this was something I could be excited about.

So I signed up, and when the day came I was actually looking forward to my three hours of labor. When I got to the nursing home, the director gave us a short orientation before we spent time with the residents. We could paint their nails, push them outside for some fresh air, or whatever we wanted to do.

"Does anyone play the piano?" the director asked.

"Me!" I said. "I play."

"We have a really nice electric piano on wheels," she said. "Would you like to push it from room to room and play for the residents?"

Briar patch. This was my briar patch.

The lady gave me a songbook from the 1950s, and for three hours, I pushed that piano from room to room, playing for the residents. One lady held up her arms and "played" the violin with me. She cried with joy over the music, and I knew the Lord had me doing good work.

When I was done, I asked the director, "May I come back again?"

For an entire year, I played weekly for the nursing

home residents. Once, I arrived to find that a resident had gathered his friends in one of the large rooms. He pulled out his violin and some of his music, and we played an entire concert together. That was some crazy hard music, and I was sweating by the time we were done. Afterward, I found out that he had played for a large symphony in New York City for years. He told me that our concert took him back to some really good days, before his wife had died, and before his body gave out on him. On the way home, I laughed out loud with the joy of it.

Maybe I wasn't lazy? Maybe I just needed to find the right place for my hands to work: pushing a piano instead of a broom.

We spent an entire week at Fairmont Hot Springs in Canada. A generous benefactor had given us her timeshare at a beautiful resort that was far above our pay grade. We did some hiking and drove to Banff for a day, and I actually got tired of saying, "This is so beautiful. This is so beautiful. This is so beautiful."

But I can't be still, and when we were in our apartment at the resort, I was working. I carried my laptop into the living room so I could write blog posts, and I spread out Spanish lessons on the table.

"I'm sorry. Do you want me to stop working on stuff?" I asked Matt, who was relaxing and watching TV one afternoon.

"As long as you make me one of your work stations, I'm happy," he said.

I always have to be working on something, and it almost always involves words. For several years, I wrote devotional study guides to go with every sermon series we had at church. I have no idea how many hundreds of hours I spent on this, as I pored over the Scripture, prayed for wisdom, wrote and rewrote.

Every spring, I wrote daily devotions for our youth to work through on their mission trip to Spokane. For several years, I taught our children in Awana, creating my own thirty-minute Bible lessons for them every week. I've also been writing devotional blogs online for the last four years.

But I never imagined that any of that counted. In my mind, I always went back to the work day at church when I felt like a lazy-good-for-nothing. I compared myself to the other people in the church who were good at cooking and cleaning and fixing and painting, and I seemed lazy compared to them. I was working hard, though. I just hadn't been able to see it.

Jesus said this about himself: "I am the way, and

the truth, and the life" (John 14:6a). I am starting to see that Jesus uses truth to show us where we should and should not carry blame. In every chapter of this book, I can see how false expectations and false labels have kept a boot on my neck, pinning me down and making me feel hopeless. Jesus is slowly lifting the lies and giving me hope that I can be a good housewife. I can be a hard worker. I can move closer to flawless living every day.

"I'm so lazy," I moaned, looking at the pile of undone dishes in the kitchen.

"You are the least lazy person I know," Matt said. I looked at him. For so long I had spit the word *loser* at myself that I could barely accept his words as true. *He doesn't know what he's talking about*, I said to myself. But what if he was right?

King Solomon speaks, on multiple occasions, about the "sluggard," and he commands: "Go to the ant, O sluggard; consider her ways, and be wise" (Proverbs 6:6). I have always preached this to myself when I feel lazy: *Go to the ant, you sluggard!* But I am learning to be kinder to myself when it comes to that label of laziness. I really do work hard. I work hard on my writing and on my Spanish lesson plans and in caring about people at church. I work hard to make sure we have clean clothes and a fairly tidy house.

Sometimes I don't work hard. Sometimes I check Facebook when I should be emptying the dishwasher. That's when I need to go to the ant and get with it. When the Spirit pricks my conscience about the dishes, it's time for me to get up and do them.

What truth do you think Jesus wants you to see about your own work ethic?

CHAPTER NINE

I'm Late, I'm Late, I'm Late

I am writing the beginning of this chapter in the house where I grew up, and I can almost hear my dad's voice booming at us to get into the car for church. Services started at eleven o'clock, and when I was growing up, he wanted us in the car and pulling out of the garage at ten thirty. The church is all of two miles from our house.

Why not leave at 10:54? That's how my thoughts ran.

I have lived with this mentality for a long time. Leaving just at the very last minute means I hug people's bumpers and curse the red lights. *Why so many red lights?* It has made me the master of excuses for being late.

"Sorry, I had to..."

"Sorry, I would have been here sooner, but..."

How is it that I was raised to be early, and still became this person who arrived just as every event began? I ran across this meme on Pinterest just today: "When you run out of excuses: 'I'm late because of who I am as a person.'" This is the key to change: telling myself the truth. When I stop blaming red lights, and admit that I am late because of my own poor time management, then shame comes in. And shame is actually a good starting place if I want to become blameless. Jesus calls it poverty of spirit, and offers me the kingdom of heaven as a reward for acknowledging my own failures.

I admitted my issues with tardiness to my mom and, endearingly, she quoted Shakespeare to me: "Better three hours too soon than a minute too late." I've done the minute-too-late thing more often than not, and it is a miserable way to live.

When I got the job teaching high school Spanish at Stillwater Christian School, I had just come out of a decade as a medical transcriptionist. In the last year of typing medical reports, I had grown tired of the unpredictable amount of work. I had also developed chronic pain in the right side of my neck, down my arm, and into my thumb, from typing eighty-some words a minute for hours every day.

I started to procrastinate typing the medical reports. And the more I procrastinated, the more I found myself submitting work in the nick of time, or an hour after the nick. (Just so you know, I haven't told anyone that my bosses had to start calling to ask where my work was. Is it stupid to write a book and tell the whole world my junk? But it seems that all my chapters begin with shame before they get to the transformation, so I continue.)

I really needed to get out of that job for the sake of my body, and I wanted out of it because of embarrassment over my increasingly slipshod work ethic. Thankfully, the government forced doctors to go electronic, so my job phased out until it was all gone. That's when God put the teaching job in my lap, and I was thrilled to do something new that would allow my body to recuperate from the repetition of typing. (Well, minus this book-writing thing, but you know.)

Sometime in those first few days of teacher

orientation, I heard someone talking about the school superintendent: "He's really a stickler for being early. He's known for saying, 'If you're not ten minutes early, you're late.'"

Great.

I see God's kindness in letting me try again at being the early employee, instead of the tardy one. It was nice to have a fresh start. So, right off the bat, I determined what time I needed to drive away from my house in order to be thirty minutes early to work. Knowing my tendency to do "one more thing" before leaving, I decided that "running late" should mean that I'm only twenty minutes early to work instead of thirty. I'm three years into this teaching job now, and I have been habitually early to work.

Thank God that in the places where we've failed, He lets us try again.

When I was in college, I went with some fellow students to help out at a church in Mexico over spring break. We drove down to the border of Texas and crossed into Nuevo Laredo by foot. It was my first trip to a foreign country, and an exciting opportunity to practice the Spanish I had been learning. (That was where I learned the difference between the Spanish phrases that mean you "like the pastor" versus you "*like* the pastor." Lord have mercy, that was an embarrassing language mistake.)

One day, with typical Latin-American hospitality, the pastor took our team to see his home. Afterward, we were getting back into the van to go to a scheduled event, when a friend of the pastor's came by. Those two men chatted for a long time, so long that I started looking at my watch. We were going to be late. And that's how I learned that in the Hispanic world, the event begins when you get there, and relationships with people trump appointment schedules.

It was my first experience in Africa, and I had everything in my backpack to teach a morning Bible study session to the Ugandan women. But the taxi driver didn't show up at our hotel until it was time for the Bible study to start. This was beyond my comprehension. We should have been at the church and teaching already.

We took the drive through "the land of potholes," as the native pastor described it. Parking on a patch of grass, we were led through what seemed like an alley for sewage drainage, and entered a rough shack that was designated as a church. The floor was dirt. Light came through the cracks in the walls and, as usual for Kampala, one light bulb hung from a wire and lit the room. There was a shiny piece of garland draped along the wall behind the podium.

My friend and I were greeted as honored guests and led past the simple wooden benches to an old but cushioned couch at the front. The young girl who had grabbed my backpack at the door knelt in front of me out of respect, and I could not breathe with the humility I felt in that moment.

There were only a few people in the church, however, and my disappointment was keen. We had made two nine-hour flights across the country for this moment, and no one had come.

Soon the female pastor started to play the drums, and a young man started singing. As we listened to this style of music that was new to me, people started arriving. One by one, women and a few men arrived, until the room was filled.

Later, I was told that people come to events when they hear the music start. This was Africa.

Americans are not called to an event when the music starts; we watch the clock. And when it comes to arriving at work, punctuality matters. In Proverbs 18:9 we read, "One who is slack in his work is brother to one who destroys." When it comes to arrival at work, "slack" is certainly not defined in the same terms in the United States as it is in Mexico and Uganda. My parents and grandparents would tell you that being anything but early to work or to events is slacking. Maybe the most flawless thing we can do sometimes is to stop and have a conversation with someone, even if it makes us late, but I think for us in the United States, being early is the greatest way to show we care about people, especially our employers.

When I grow up (I'm shooting for this to occur in my fifties now), I hope I'm like my mother-in-law and her sister. When we meet them at any event, we know they are going to be half an hour early – or earlier. And they're busy ladies with full days. It's the mindset of the generation that went before me, I think. I doubt either of my parents were ever late for work a single day of their lives, and I wonder why this good habit didn't seem to transfer to me.

There was one time I was early.

We got married on a Saturday, and I pushed hard for us to go to church the next day. My husband rolled his eyes, but he honored my request. We left our cozy hotel room, with the river rock fireplace that took up one entire wall, and headed to the little Southern Baptist church in Jackson Hole, Wyoming.

When we got there, the parking lot was empty.

Then one of us realized that we had never changed our clocks from Texas time, so we had arrived an hour before church began. My new husband was super excited that he had not only gotten ready for church not even twenty-four hours into his honeymoon, but he had also lost an hour of sleep in the bargain.

We decided to make the best of it, though, and he took me for a big breakfast. Then we went to church on Wyoming time. I don't know why we even bothered attending, because these two little girls sat in front of us and worked to pull a loose tooth from one of their mouths. This went on for almost the entire sermon, until finally the one little girl gasped and ran for the bathroom with a bloody tooth in her hand. Please do not ask me what the pastor said that day.

So anyway, I was early. An hour early.

I think my husband wishes he could have kept our clocks an hour early for the rest of our marriage. He really likes to leave early for things, which I think is a time waster when you could be tasking yourself to the last second, but it makes him crazy when I'm always running late for events.

I found I was always trying to beat his phone call as I drove to church. "Oh, shoot. That's your dad," I would say to the kids.

"Are you coming?" he would ask.

"I'm here! I'm in the parking lot," I would say to him, as if I totally had my act together and it wasn't a big deal that he was starting to give up on me.

I'm still not the best at it, but I've been trying really hard to be early to church. It stresses Matt when I'm late, and sometimes he needs my help with something before the service. Like the important job of paper-clipping his microphone cord to his T-shirt. (Pastor's wife: not a role everyone is equipped to fill.)

Paul says, "Wives, submit to your own husbands, as to the Lord" (Ephesians 5:22). The Spirit of God has increasingly been prompting me to submit to Matt's desire for me to come early to church. Tardiness may not matter so much to a husband in Nuevo Laredo or Uganda, but it matters to this Montana guy.

When I arrive half an hour early for work, I enter the school at a relaxed pace. I walk into the office area and check my mail box, and I'm not annoyed if the secretary or a teacher chats with me for a few minutes, because I'm not in a hurry.

I get my room set up for the day, which leaves time for a trip to the ice machine to fill my water bottle. I go over my lesson plans and rethink some things, making some good last-minute changes. There is time to neatly arrange supplies on the left corner of my desk, and even time to get started on some work for the future, or to grade a few papers. The bell rings, and I feel ready to stand and greet students as if they're coming into my home.

I never thought I would be able to say that I am consistently early to a job. There used to be slack in my work, as I was sliding in on the seat of my pants, but God disciplined me out of that habit. I am starting to experience how this work ethic of timeliness is a gift to my students, and to my daily blood pressure.

❖

I finished writing this grand chapter of wisdom about punctuality yesterday, and you would not believe what happened today, not even twenty-four hours later.My daughter is home for Easter weekend, and we made plans to see *Cinderella* with my mother-in-law and her sister. (I made Jayme promise she would never grow out of watching Disney princess movies with me.)

The movie start time was 11:50. Since I had just written about promptness, I told Jayme I would pick her up at 11:00. That would get us to the theater in time to chat with Barb and Joan for twenty minutes before the movie started.

But I did my normal "one more task," and found myself leaving the house at 10:57, which was seven minutes late. Not that big a deal, except on my way out I saw the vest that needed to be dry-cleaned. I thought, *Why not?* So I texted my daughter that I was leaving late and stopping in at the dry cleaners.

All I know is that I found myself sweating with anxiety about being late, feeling rushed in traffic, and thinking of excuses to give my mother-in-law.

Same.

Old.

Story.

After I stepped on my mother's toes (literally and figuratively, it would seem), we sat down in our theater seats, just two minutes before the lights dimmed and the movie trailers began. When the king said to his son, "Punctuality is the politeness of princes," my guilty conscience put the thumbscrews to me, and I groaned out loud in the theater. I felt ashamed of my immaturity in managing my time.

When we got home from the theater, my son asked what twist they added to the plot to make the retelling of *Cinderella* interesting.

"No twist," we said.

"Then what's the point? You mean it was exactly the same?" he asked.

"Yeah, exactly the same," we said. "Cinderella gets the prince. Why would anyone change that?"

He shook his head at me.

Disney knows not to mess with a good thing, and *Cinderella* is the perfect story to watch right after you've blown it. The great prince sweeps in, just in the nick of time, and rescues the lowly servant girl. Even though she isn't worthy of him, she gets to go to the palace: fantastic and cinder-free, new wardrobe included. Happily ever after.

And so I have hope that Jesus will continue to rescue me and dress me in new robes of punctuality. To live happily (and on time) ever after.

CHAPTER TEN

THROW IT OFF

Every spring, our workout facility hosts a 5K called the Summit Classic. I have walked it before, coming in ten minutes behind the rest of my family, which means they ran, cooled down, and then got comfortable on a curb to wait for their momma who should stick to reading books.

My son was in middle school when he and his buddies signed up for the Summit Classic, and they trained hard. We heard my son's archless feet slapping on the treadmill every night for a few weeks, until he got his practice time down to an impressive number. He was ready to take the lead.

The day of the 5K dawned typically for Kalispell in the spring: cold and rainy. In April, the real, you-can-feel-it spring is still a long, long way away. (The men at Hooper's Garden Center post a sign warning you not to even *think* about planting flowers outside until the snow has melted off Columbia Mountain, which we all know is going to take its time and slowly run into the rivers come late May.)

The race was in the morning, and I was thinking how smart I was to be the momma who would just stand and cheer for the boys at the starting line, and then go sip a hot beverage in the truck with the heater running until it was time for them to cross the finish line.

Soon he was off and running. Then I was watching his gang cross the finish line one by one. No Caleb. I really expected him much sooner, perhaps even ahead of his friends. Finally, I saw him half-walking and half-running, hands holding his sides, and a look of pain on his face.

My boy was not happy, completely humiliated and frustrated at his slow time. We couldn't figure out what the problem was.

Until he took off his sweatshirt and handed it to me.

He had worn that sweatshirt while they waited

for the race to start. He had worn it the whole time he ran, and, with each minute in the rain, his shirt gained weight. I bet it weighed ten pounds, and he didn't train with an extra ten pounds slogging against his back while he ran.

Many, many years ago there was a time when we had these things called cameras. We put a little tube called "film" in the camera. After we took twelve or twenty-four or thirty-six pictures, we removed the film, drove to the store, and paid to have it developed into these things called "pictures," which meant the faces of our friends and family printed on paper. Actual paper that we could tape to the frig.

The cool girls put those special paper memories into scrapbooks. The not-cool girls put theirs into photo albums with sticky paper pages. We super artsy overachiever types spent an exorbitant amount of money on scrapbook supplies.

When my daughter was born, I attended a Creative Memories party and was sold. I would be the scrapbooking mom. The only problem was our poverty versus the cost of the hobby. Thankfully, Mom loved the scrapbooking supplies, so she started funding a big part of it, vicariously enjoying the craft without actually putting in the hours of labor cropping pictures (with actual scissors) and making pretty frames for the photos on the page.

Every year I made a scrapbook of family pictures, and they were pretty cool. We love to pull them out with our now-grown kids and look back at the memories that I documented.

Sometime around year twelve of scrapbooking, I started to notice something about my thoughts: They were consumed with making scrapbooks. I was a busy mom with young kids, and I was constantly trying to think how I could keep them occupied so I could put pictures in the book. (Does anyone else see anything wrong with that?) More than that, I was obsessed with how I could possibly afford to buy more supplies. We were so very broke and barely able to pay bills and buy groceries. If it weren't for generous grandmas, my kids would have been naked.

But how could I get more scrapbook supplies?

The writer of Hebrews gives a specific instruction for those who are running after Christ. "Therefore, since we are surrounded by so great a cloud of witnesses, let us also lay aside every weight, and sin which clings so closely, and let us run with endurance the race that is set before us" (Hebrews 12:1).

Scrapbooking was not a sin, but I was ashamed of my hobby. It was starting to consume more of my thoughts and energy than I was investing in my relationships with Christ and with my family.

Though I had been determined to scrapbook for the rest of my life, I decided to finish the scrapbook I was on, and then be done with that hobby. It had become like the sweatshirt my son wore in the 5K, slowly soaking up my time and energy and keeping me from more important work. Like spending time with the people in the pictures.

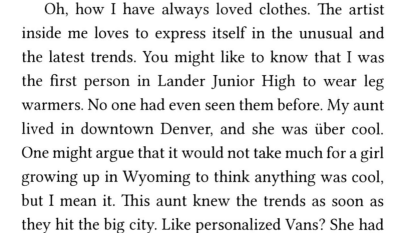

Oh, how I have always loved clothes. The artist inside me loves to express itself in the unusual and the latest trends. You might like to know that I was the first person in Lander Junior High to wear leg warmers. No one had even seen them before. My aunt lived in downtown Denver, and she was über cool. One might argue that it would not take much for a girl growing up in Wyoming to think anything was cool, but I mean it. This aunt knew the trends as soon as they hit the big city. Like personalized Vans? She had some Vans airbrushed with a piano keyboard for me, and I was something in those shoes. I was something.

That enjoyment of clothing has never changed. I'll probably be eighty years old and saying, "Hey, check out my bell bottoms." (I'm just guessing on the bell bottoms. Hopefully I'll be in heaven with Jesus before they cycle into the height of fashion again.) But we've never had any money for clothes. For the basics, yes, but not enough money to satisfy my really great taste. So pretty much every day, I would open the closet doors and sigh.

Nothing to wear.

"Nothing" meant *Nothing new and beautiful and wow-the-crowd to wear.*

Every day, I struggled with dissatisfaction in what I was wearing, my spirit longing for constantly new and varied beautiful clothing. But then I did two things. I started reading true stories about people around the world, sometimes in *National Geographic* and sometimes in autobiographies and biographies, and I began to see poverty on the page. Also, I took a trip to Uganda.

One day in Uganda, I was waiting by the car for a while, and I watched a mom in her little hut where she worked all day for maybe one dollar. She was playing with her baby, who was clothed in a T-shirt. No diaper. No pants. No matching Gymboree socks and hat.

After that trip, I began to feel ashamed when I

opened my closet door – not ashamed of my clothes, but ashamed at my lack of gratitude for having clothes. I would go to pick a shirt and wish I had a new one, only to realize that I had to *choose* a shirt to wear. I had a choice, and choices mean wealth.

One day, I decided that I was going to live gratefully and keep in mind the poverty of the rest of the world. At that time, I was chafing at the fact that I owned only two pairs of pants. I decided that for one year I would trade off wearing those two pairs of pants, purposefully refusing to buy more.

Jesus says, "Life is more than food, and the body more than clothing" (Luke 12:23). If I was going to be able to feel good in my soul at the end of the day, I needed to stave off my appetite for looking fashionable.

I still love clothes: the expensive kind. But I threw off the hobby of accumulating new clothes so I could make room in my heart for compassion. I needed to get dressed every morning with a thankful heart, and let my worry be for the people who lacked even proper covering for their bodies.

One time, someone asked me about my hobbies. "Reading," I replied.

"And?" she said.

"And what?" I said. "I read books. That's it."

Now, let me tell you that I was always at the bottom of the magazine chain. My grandma bought magazines of all kinds: cooking magazines, house décor magazines, women's magazines. She looked at them, and then when we went to visit her, my mom would come home with a brown paper sack full of magazines. She would look at them, and then they would come to me. I definitely didn't have money in my budget for splurging on magazines, so this was a special treat.

One day, I picked up one of the magazines, and there was a mouth-watering entrée pictured on the front cover. I slowly perused the pages, until I came to the spot where that recipe should have been. Except it wasn't there, because someone in the magazine hierarchy thought it looked really good, too, and had taken scissors to that page. Hmmph.

I spent a lot of time looking at magazines, until I began feeling empty when I looked at them. Empty and unsatisfied. Empty and wanting more.

I do things abruptly. Like the one day I stopped scrapbooking, and the one day I decided to wear two pairs of pants for a year, on this day I decided I needed to read more wisely. The magazines were fun, but I was feeling ashamed at the amount of time I was spending with my face in them, when I could be reading something that would make my soul richer.

That's when I started checking out dusty missionary books from the church library. I put down novels and magazines, and picked up nonfiction books that were meant to help a follower of Christ live for Christ.

Today is the first day of my spring break from teaching, and I am reading a novel for fun. I also have some hand-me-down magazines in a little basket by my living room couch. Sometimes it's nice to relax and look at pretty pictures. But most of my reading time is now very purposeful, and I can feel how people's real-life stories of following God are building up inside me.

Now that I am a devotional writer, I can see how God moved in my heart to make this shift in reading, so that I always have a rich pool of thoughts for writing. Jesus says, "The good person out of the good treasure of his heart produces good, and the evil person out of his evil treasure produces evil, for out of the abundance of the heart his mouth speaks" (Luke 6:45). I needed to store up knowledge so I would have good things to share with other people.

My husband went on a trip to Spokane with some friends from church, so they could run the popular Bloomsday race, in which more than 50,000 people participate. Of course, I stayed home and read books.

Matt had a lot of fun running, but he came home talking about memorable experiences that didn't include the athletic part of the race. He told me about how cold it was in the early morning before the race began and how, when people started running, they pulled off their warm outer clothing and threw it on the side of the road. He found this shocking, until he learned that a local organization comes by afterward and takes all the clothing to help those in need. Apparently people in Spokane know that when a race begins, you take off the weighty clothing and get down to the light athletic gear.

Then Matt told me about the leg of the race where he was losing his wind, and felt that maybe he wasn't going to make it. About that time, he passed some bystanders, and a little girl yelled to him, "Your momma's gonna be so proud of you!" That cheer touched his heart and kept him going hard for the rest of the race.

It's ridiculous for a bookworm to use this whole running analogy, but I ran once, so I feel like I can.

As a follower of Christ, I am running a race, and

I want to run in light clothing – nothing weighing me down or hindering me from doing well. I want Jesus to be so proud of me. That means getting rid of habits and hobbies in my life that aren't necessarily bad, but which take brain power, money, and energy that could be invested in more eternal purposes.

CHAPTER ELEVEN

CREDIT CHECK

A few years past Matt getting his master's degree, and with two little kids, we were anxious to buy our first home. We knew we had a meager income and would need something older and small, but it didn't matter to us. Gathering paperwork, we went to our first-ever appointment with a mortgage company.

The lady was very nice and asked us a lot of questions, but then came the question that made me sick to my stomach: "What kind of debt do you have?"

We both graduated debt-free with our bachelor's degrees, but then we had piled up loans with Matt's master's. I was humiliated by our debt, which made me feel like a failure and a "slave of the lender" (Proverbs 22:7).

"We owe sixteen thousand dollars in school loans," I said, cowering in my chair.

She stared at me for a minute, and I knew I deserved the incredulous look she was giving me. "Wow," she said. "I wish all of my clients walked in here with that small a debt."

It was my turn to sport an incredulous look.

Thousands of dollars in debt, and we were the good example of money management? That fact was horrifying to me, and I determined in my heart that, Lord willing, someday we would be shameless in how we handled our money.

Ten years. That's how long it took us to pay off Matt's student loans. That was ten years of me looking at the checkbook every day. Ten years of trying to figure out how to make the loan payment, and buy groceries. Ten years of having no clothing budget, and crying with relief when someone gave us hand-me-downs. Ten years with no savings account to cover emergency expenses. Ten years of depending on the generosity of parents or on credit cards to get us out of a hole.

Ten years of slavery.

And every single day for ten years, I prayed. I

dripped tears over the checkbook, and asked God if He would help us to honor Him by helping us shake the debt. "We don't need to be rich," I prayed. "We don't need vacations or fancy clothes. Please, Lord, just help us get free from the credit cards and the school loans."

Every day, I kneeled at the throne of heaven and begged.

His name was Larry Burkett, and he is in heaven with Jesus now. But before he shook the dust off his shoes here, he helped me so much. I listened to him on the radio and got *The Financial Planning Workbook.* I learned how to make a budget, which was a new thought to me.

Let me pause here to say that my parents were incredible with money, and Dad passed that wisdom down to me. I don't know why it didn't stick. Maybe I wasn't really open to practicing it when he was saying it? I don't know. But while I wish I could go back and do things Dad's way from the beginning, God was kind enough to keep sending me money knowledge until I reached out and grabbed it.

I made a budget, but learning to live by it was like a little kid trying to learn how to ride a bike: wobbly, followed by crash and burn, then get up and try again. I started to get a handle on where our money was going, though, and in my heart I wanted to spend every penny in a way that would make God happy.

Mr. Burkett talked about saving one thousand dollars to use for emergencies. You have no idea how impossible that seemed when we barely had money for necessities, and for debt payments that wouldn't stop. A thousand dollars in savings was the Everest of money goals at that time, but I started by tucking three dollars into that account, sometimes six dollars, but rarely more than ten, until one day we had that one thousand dollars in emergency savings.

That's when everything changed. With a cushion in place for the unexpected expenses, we started putting that three and six and ten dollars extra toward the student loans and the Visa bill.

One day we had friends over. I pulled out a bottle of the good stuff (sparkling cider), and we filled glasses, walked across the street to the mailboxes, and celebrated our last payment to the student loan company. Our consumer debt was gone.

Okay, so there's one lesson from Dad I got loud

and clear. He gave ten percent of his income to the Lord's work. Well, I know it was much more than ten percent when you add all he and Mom gave to church family and to missionaries, but it was the ten percent that Dad preached. "We give off the top to the Lord first," he would always say.

It really was a gift to have been raised this way. From the time I did my first babysitting job, I had an envelope in my room marked "offering." I would cash the check and put ten percent into that envelope. I imagine those who come to know God later in life really struggle with giving up a huge chunk of income for kingdom work, and I'm thankful Dad made this a nonnegotiable for me.

But when you love the Lord, ten percent seems paltry.

Again, Larry Burkett taught me about living for the kingdom of God. He taught me to spend less and less on self, and more and more on sharing the good news of Jesus and helping the poor.

So in the Word document that sports our budget, I drew a line between our expenses and what I titled "Kingdom Work." I used a huge font size to make that heading, and in my heart I planted my feet on this line. I made a private rule for myself: Once I put an amount below the line, it stayed there, with

God's help. Over the years, we slowly dropped new charitable contributions below the line.

I once heard someone say that to look at a person's check register is to see where the treasure of her heart is placed. When I die, I want someone to look at my check register and see that my husband and I lived on very little, and spent a ridiculous amount of money on stuff that matters to God.

A dozen years ago, we moved out of our old starter home into a beautiful new home that was made possible only by the grace of God. Our neighbors built their house not long after we did, so we were landscaping our yards at the same time.

Our neighbors planted sod. And put up a vinyl fence. And planted trees.

We could afford food and our mortgage and not much else, so we scraped together money for grass seed, and as the lawn began to grow, Matt made us all go out and pull ten weeds every day. "Come on, little grass seed," we said, as we hosted a small party for every precious new blade of grass.

We couldn't help but compare our sad attempts at landscaping to our neighbor's rich strides forward.

How can they have so much money to do all that? I wondered.

Then I remembered the line. The kingdom line. They didn't have one of those.

I remembered my shame over our debt and how God had freed us in answer to my prayers. It has been more than a dozen years since we paid off the final school loans and credit cards, and we haven't had consumer debt since. How can I even begin to show my gratitude to God?

Did I want to fund sod or missionary work around the world? I would be content with grass seed.

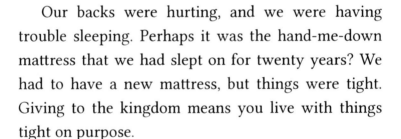

Our backs were hurting, and we were having trouble sleeping. Perhaps it was the hand-me-down mattress that we had slept on for twenty years? We had to have a new mattress, but things were tight. Giving to the kingdom means you live with things tight on purpose.

One day, we got a flier in the mail that advertised an incredible mattress sale at the furniture store just down the road from us. They also had zero percent financing for six months. We knew we could pay off the mattress in two months, so we decided to go for it.

I went to the furniture store, chose the mattress, and waited at the counter while they did the financing paperwork. "I'm just waiting for your credit score," the lady said. When it came through, I asked her what it was. She read me a number in the high seven hundreds.

I may have internally busted into a little dance that I could not keep from reaching my face.

"That's really high," she said.

"Yeah," I replied, all nonchalant. As I'm writing this, I'm ashamed that I didn't give God the glory for that number while I was at the furniture store that day. But I'm giving Him glory now. For ten years I prayed. Ten years of shame. But look what God has done in my life: He brought me out of financial shame and into a place where I can hold up my head.

<hr />

It was time to gather paperwork for taxes, which is mostly depressing when you get to the bracket where you're paying in and not getting anything back.

We started getting tax-related mail in January: W-2s and all that. But we also received several financial statements about our charitable giving. One was from the church, and it had a number on it that would have made my dad proud. I thought back to my jealous moments over the neighbors' landscaping, and years of watching them accumulate expensive toys. The church giving record was an ultrasound of my heart.

Then other records started to arrive from places where we've given so people can receive physical assistance and hear about Jesus. These were the kinds of papers I wanted to carry to the tax man.

Matt got a cost-of-living raise just about the time the Compassion International representatives made their plea. I had been watching people sponsor children through Compassion for years and had been secretly jealous of them. I couldn't imagine us being able to add that expense to our budget every month.

But that preacher man and I were sitting on the front row when the couple spoke about sponsoring a Compassion child, and I wanted this so badly. I looked at Matt. He looked at me, and he gave me a smile and nod of permission. It was all I could do to sit through the rest of the evening service.

After church, I went and stood in front of the Compassion tables. From the spread-out packets of information, faces of all colors and nationalities looked at us, and I thought my heart would break with the joy and the pain of it. So many in need.

Matt came up beside me.

"You pick," I said.

He looked for a few minutes, until his eyes came to the round four-year-old face of Haydy from Colombia. Her eyes were big, and we could see the still-baby dimples in her hands.

"Her," he said. "And she's from a Spanish-speaking country, so that's perfect for us." We have both worked to learn the Spanish language, and we have many Hispanic friends.

We were in love with this little girl. It was an adoption of sorts.

I took the packet, and Matt moved away to greet our church family as they came out of the sanctuary. Sitting down at the table to fill out the paperwork, I opened my checkbook and started crying like a fool. The couple looked at me from behind the table, a little dismayed at my tears. Finally collecting myself, I said, "You have no idea how long I've wanted to help this little girl. This is a dream come true for me."

Haydy feels like part of our family now. I send her Hello Kitty coloring pages and stickers. We pray for her and her parents when we ask the blessing over dinner. We pray the Lord will protect her within her impoverished, dangerous community. We pray she will come to know Jesus – she and her mom and dad.

Now when things get tight, I still pray over my checkbook, but God has transformed the prayer of shame over debt into a prayer of pleading on behalf of Haydy. *Lord, please provide what we need to live, so that we never have to remove her name from below the kingdom line of our budget.*

Our 401(k) is pathetic and our savings are still humble. We don't go on expensive vacations or buy fancy clothes. Our cars are old. We make no home improvements except for necessary maintenance. But we are putting more and more money into God's kingdom work.

And I've never felt so good about our finances.

CHAPTER TWELVE

KEEPING CHRISTMAS

He and his wife were visiting our church around Christmas time. To make them feel welcome, I struck up a conversation, and soon we were talking about all things Christmas.

"Our family no longer gives Christmas gifts to each other," he said. "We look for ways to give to those in need, instead of focusing on ourselves at Christmas. It's the best choice we have ever made."

Enter: Shame.

I was already questioning the way we celebrated Christmas. Our kids were young, and I was considering what kind of traditions we should be setting in place for our family. Because I am a person of extremes, I began to think that we were simply heathens for the grandiose way we celebrated Christmas, with our bulging, overflowing stockings and piles of gifts under the tree.

I kept shopping, as was Christmas tradition, but I felt sinful in doing so. Surely we were disappointing God on His own special holiday. But what could I do against such a mighty Christmas engine? The season began to be drudgery for me, as I thought about how horrible we were for storing up treasures for ourselves at Christmas.

My dad knew how to give good gifts. Because of his generosity, I was able to accept that God is generous and extravagant in His love for us. I know these things about God partly because of what Christmas was like at my house when I was growing up. I saw the delight in my dad's eyes when he would surprise us with a dream-come-true gift. In those generous, indulgent moments, I became convinced that I could present my requests to God and know that He wanted to lavish His love on me by caring for all of my needs.

It was a special Christmas. Matt received unexpected payment for some counseling he had done, and at first I considered a list of practical ways we could use that money. After some thought, though, I went to the bank and cashed that check in hundred-dollar bills. On the bank envelope, I wrote, "Shouldn't a man sometimes get to enjoy the money he earns and spend it however he wants?" Then I slipped the envelope into Matt's drawer in the kitchen.

So Matt went shopping.

He splurged on his co-workers. He splurged on me. He splurged on the kids. I gulped down thoughts about how we could have spent that money "wisely." But he was so happy.

Then my preacher man got up to preach during that Christmas season, and he opened his sermon by talking about how much he loves Christmas, because he loves spoiling his kids. He preached about how Christmas just seems to be the time when you can't help giving.

As he preached, I saw it again: the look on a dad's face when he could bring joy to his kids by giving them extravagant presents.

"If you then, who are evil, know how to give good

gifts to your children, how much more will your Father who is in heaven give good things to those who ask him!" (Matthew 7:11).My heart. Oh, my heart on that night.

Was it possibly okay for us to have one time a year when we poured out our love on our kids in a frivolous, we-love-you way? Could that be pleasing to the Lord?

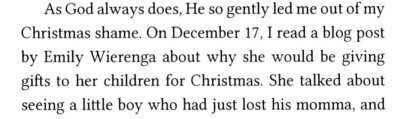

As God always does, He so gently led me out of my Christmas shame. On December 17, I read a blog post by Emily Wierenga about why she would be giving gifts to her children for Christmas. She talked about seeing a little boy who had just lost his momma, and right then she decided she would give gifts to her sons while she could. I may have bawled at the computer.

I thought of the years when I had slowly grown more judgmental toward my family and what I declared to be their Christmas materialism, and God whispered to my heart, *What a precious gift, to receive something thoughtful and hand-wrapped by your mother.*

In the year that God was talking to me about Christmas, my own dad went to heaven. The same year in which Emily wrote that note about how special it is for our children to receive gifts from their parents. How I will miss seeing the look on Dad's face as I open a special gift from him.

The same God who said, "Don't store up treasures for yourselves" also said, "If you then, though you are evil, know how to give good gifts to your children, how much more..."

How much more.

"How much more will your Father in heaven give good gifts."

I saw the look of childlike joy on my husband's face while he was preaching, and I'm the only one in the congregation who knew how happy it made him to blow through a healthy stack of Benjamin Franklins on behalf of the people he loves. In that moment I felt the gospel deep in my soul.

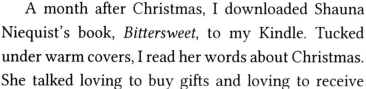

A month after Christmas, I downloaded Shauna Niequist's book, *Bittersweet*, to my Kindle. Tucked under warm covers, I read her words about Christmas. She talked loving to buy gifts and loving to receive gifts.

As I read those words, I felt the Father reach out

His hand to me and say, *Let's step out of the shame that has surrounded Christmas, shall we?*

I thought of this verse: "How great is the love the Father has lavished on us, that we should be called children of God!" (1 John 3:1 NIV)

I began to understand that lavish giving is straight from God's heart.

Our church had adopted a low-income apartment complex, and our family chose to share Christmas with a twenty-year-old woman who lived in those apartments. I took Jayme shopping with me and gave her no limit. This grown daughter of mine was in college and could barely afford food, let alone Christmas gifts, but no one loves to help the poor more than my girl. I knew this shopping trip would, in itself, be a Christmas gift to my Jayme.

Grabbing a cart, we relished a long hour in T.J. Maxx. We labored over the choice of a winter hat, and then selected some warm socks and a scarf. We bought "smell good," as my grandma would say. Then we worked our way through Christmas decorations, snack foods, paper products, and kitchen gadgets. The total at the register made me gasp for a second.It was expensive. And wonderful.

When we got home, Jayme put her artistic skills to work and filled the pretty basket we had bought. It was so full that she had to remove some items from their packaging, to make it all fit. We imagined together how happy the young woman would be when she unpacked, and unpacked, and unpacked her Christmas basket. Would she feel the love of God pouring over her?

We so hoped she would feel the love of God.

My mother gave me the loveliest copy of *A Christmas Carol* by Charles Dickens. Hardback even, like rich people read. And I opened it and sniffed the inside, before I lay down on the couch next to Matt so I could join him in reading.

Just the two of us next to the electric fireplace, Christmas decorations newly up and flameless candles flickering on the windowsill next to the wise men (because I stage a yearly revolt in refusing to put the wise men, unbiblically, at the manger).

And so I began reading in the quiet of the evening. Until I made it through the first sentence and let out a musical sigh of delight. "Oh Matthew, this first sentence is extraordinary. Listen: 'Marley was dead, to begin with.'" If you have not sat down to write the first sentence of a story, you cannot imagine how much respect I have for Mr. Dickens' striking beginning.

My darling turned from his novel to humor me with his caring. "Yes, a wonderful sentence."

"Oh, sorry," I said. Because it's so annoying when you're reading and someone starts talking to you. So I continued on until the end of paragraph three, when I groaned like I was taking my first bite of my friend's homemade pumpkin cupcake with salted caramel cream cheese frosting.

"Oh Matthew, Dickens spent one entire paragraph explaining why he *had* to use the cliché 'dead as a door-nail.' He said if he did not use the cliché 'dead as a door-nail' then 'the Country's done for.'"

My husband made an *I-love-you-but-if-you-interrupt-me-again* face, but before he turned back to his own book, he looked over my shoulder at the page and asked, "Why did Dickens capitalize 'Country'?"

"Because a cliché would ruin the whole country," I said. "Can you imagine spending a whole paragraph justifying your use for a cliché? Magnificent."

I was pushing marriage to its limits, so I lay down with my head on Matt's leg and read, ever so quietly. I even got to the second page. But an entire paragraph describing Scrooge's internal temperature? "Oh

Matthew!"

He grabbed the book from my hand and read that very paragraph in his best radio theater voice, and I will deeply love him for this –forever and all eternity.

"I'll never write as well as Charles Dickens," I said. (See how I said "well" there instead of "good"?)

Matt said "No, you will not, because Charles Dickens lived in the 1800s." And I don't know how that is an encouraging answer.

"What if I write *about* Charles Dickens?" I said.

He agreed that would make me an amazing writer, so here I am. And this is a ridiculous story, but I am giving you a glimpse through our front window, to see the great secrets of successful marriage.

Now. Ahem. Here is the truth about Scrooge, so that we may not be like him: "He carried his own low temperature always about with him; he iced his office in the dog-days and didn't thaw it one degree at Christmas."

When you read the word "iced" did you accidentally read the word "coffee" after that? "He was a squeezing, wrenching, grasping, scraping, clutching, covetous, old sinner! Hard and sharp as flint, from which no steel had ever struck out generous fire."

We carry our own temperature with us, as well. (All this heart-temperature talk is easier to appreciate if you live in Montana, where we are excited if it has warmed up to twenty degrees in the winter.)

I find myself sitting up during the end of the story, as Dickens forces us to use our imaginations, picturing how the Cratchit family reacted to such a surprising gift. *Yes, this is good!* I sing to myself. Who would dare be grumpy at Scrooge for buying the prize turkey and having it sent to Bob Cratchit? Who would think him a heathen for paying the boy a generous two shillings for running the errand? Scrooge's heart has warmed, and he can't help himself.

We show the temperature of our hearts all year long. For twelve months, we give to the poor. We take meals to the hungry and find some way to bring hope to the orphans and oppressed. We deny ourselves certain luxuries, so we can support a crisis pregnancy center with that money instead. Or write a check to a missionary. Or build a home for a poor family in Mexico.

But I will no longer try to hold back a show of love for my kids at Christmas. I pray our kids will one day look back at their overflowing stockings and trust that if we loved them in such a frivolous, lavish way, surely God does too.

CHAPTER THIRTEEN

LINE RAGE

It was a hot summer day, and I was sitting in a high school classroom listening to my driver's education instructor.

He said, "You are not to exceed the speed limit when passing a car."

I furrowed my brow and tried to figure that out. How could you pass a car if you didn't go over the speed limit? It didn't make sense, but I didn't care enough to ask for an explanation.

I was several years into driving as an adult when understanding came to me one day, as I was passing a car on the highway and going well over the speed limit. *Oh, I get it. If a car in front of you is going the speed limit, there's no need to pass.* Except I was raised by my lead-footed father, who infused in me the concept that a car should be passed so that it's not in front of you any longer.

◦──❖──◦

I was probably fifth in line, and the complaining one was probably eighth, that day at the Town Pump when I was waiting at the register to pay for my fuel. The poor girl behind the counter was frazzled. It was late afternoon rush hour at the gas station, and she was the only cashier.

"Oh, come on! How long does it take?" said the complaining woman loudly. "Could you be any slower? I'm never going to get through this line."

My shoulders tightened as I saw the discomfort on the cashier's face.

"Am I going to be here all day?" asked the complaining one.

No one in line responded.

I didn't say anything, but I thought a lot. I looked at the cashier. I turned around and looked at the complaining one, in unbelief at the ugly impatience issuing from her mouth at regular intervals. God was there, talking to me hard and fast about how I was

152

going to behave differently.

When I reached the cashier, I schooled myself to act as though I was the only one in line, and as if she was the most valuable person on earth.

"Hello!" I said cheerfully. She looked up with a weary smile.

"You doin' okay?" I asked, trying to give her an *I'm-sorry-that-lady-is-being-a-jerk-and-I-hope-you-know-you-don't-deserve-that* look. I casually paid for my fuel, and told the cashier I hoped she had a good afternoon.

When I walked out of the gas station, I was a different person.

<hr/>

In high school, I often accompanied the choirs on the piano. There was one concert in which another student came up to play the next song after me. The second my song was over, this girl came up on my left, slid onto the bench and bumped me off it with her hip.

It makes me laugh to think of it now, because it was so ridiculously rude and self-centered of her. At the time, I thought my quiet little mother was going to come unglued, and she's not the type to unglue. Let's all stop and imagine the quiet librarian lady delivering a right upper cut to the impatient pianist with the forceful hip.

If that girl could have just been patient for five seconds.

Doorways are perhaps my biggest challenge. You know how sometimes you can see that you're doing the wrong thing, as plain as day, but you're in the middle of doing it when you gain this awareness, and it's too late to go back and be a better person?

Well, first let me tell you what kind of a person I am: driven. The other day, I was walking down the hall at church, headed for a meeting. As I came through the doorway, my husband said, "Yup, I knew that was my wife. She is a person who walks with a purpose."

I'm just like my dad. He would invite me to go downtown for an errand, we would park, and he would be out of the truck and halfway down the sidewalk before I was barely stepping onto the sidewalk. "Hurry up," he would call over his shoulder. "I ain't waitin' for ya."

He loved me, but Dad was always a man on a mission that couldn't wait. Now I am a woman on a mission. I often find myself breathing heavily with the intensity of whatever I'm working at, even folding laundry, and I realize it's ridiculous. I try to relax, but it's hard.

So that brings me back to doorways and how I approach them. I walk fast, throw open the door, and plow toward whatever important something I'm going to. That's not a problem until I am approaching the door at the same time as someone else. Then there is a collision of the massive importance of my driving purpose, and the safety and value of the approaching person. Over and over, I have found myself inwardly racing to get to the door first, because *I am going somewhere,* for Pete's sake! It's embarrassing to think about. But then, this is a book about how I used to be ashamed, and how God is slowly making me a better person.

Thank God for the horrid lady at the gas station, and for His lesson to me that day on the repulsive nature of impatience and hurry. Memories of that day still affect my door approach. Although I still come up to a door full speed ahead, inside my soul the Holy Spirit of God is like Spiderman holding back the train so it doesn't go off the edge of the track. *Slow up, slow up,* He says to me. *Let the other person get through, and treat her like she's valuable.*

Spiderman barely escaped with his life on that one.

There is a very busy intersection down the road from our house. It's a single-lane intersection, but there is enough room for going straight and for drivers to sneak up on the right to turn. I always park myself in the center of that space so no one can get by me. (I hate to admit that this is partly because I'm a strong-willed child who wants to take control, but that might need to be an additional chapter, and this book is already plenty long with confessions.)

One day I was stopped in the center of the lane – and it's a long light, by the way. I heard honking from behind me, and when I looked in my rearview mirror, the people in the car behind me were leaning out of their windows, cussing at me for taking up the space, and throwing me the finger. Did I mention that it's a long light? By the time the light turned green, I felt like I had been assaulted.

The Lord spoke to my heart that day. Our culture is angry and impatient, and growing more so all the time. I can be a light in this dark world by waiting patiently when it is my turn to wait.

Possibly the DMV was created by Satan himself.

It's a bad sign when you arrive to see people slouching in rows of chairs, and you have to go past their death-camp faces to take a number from the round, red gadget hanging on the wall.

I got my number (3,467,842, or so it seemed when the lady called "Number twenty-seven"). I knew I was going to be in the waiting room for a long, long time, possibly until I had become a great-grandmother.

But I was learning how to wait, so I started talking to the Lord. He brought to mind a verse I had read that morning, and I started meditating on the truth of it. Soon I felt like the DMV had become a sanctuary, and I was having the sweetest time of prayer and worship with God. I kept praying, and kept thinking about Him, and He was talking to me through His word. On one hand, it felt magnificent, like I was in a cathedral, and on the other hand intimate, like I was in a coffee shop.

I started to look around the room, and I was seeing the people. I was seeing them the way God sees them. Each one valuable. Each one with a story. I felt love for them.

I waited a long time, but it didn't feel like it. When

my number was called, it felt like an intrusion into something sacred.

Like a complete idiot, I went to Costco at two o'clock on a Saturday afternoon. When it takes you five minutes just to maneuver around the people in the parking lot, you know you should have gone home and come back another time.

But we were out of coffee creamer, so this was emergency shopping.

I grabbed a cart and headed towards the store, while digging my Costco card out of my purse. I looked up to see an elderly man planted dead center in the entrance. With shaky fingers, he was also searching for his Costco card. Because of where he was standing, no one could get around him with their carts.

I could feel the rising tide of people behind and around me. Their impatience was palpable, and I was afraid for this man. So I pulled my cart in right behind him, took a deep breath, and gave him the grace of waiting for as long as he needed: waiting with love. I felt like a buffer between him and the must-get-in-there crowd behind me.

Once he finally found his card, his shuffling gait was painfully slow, and it still took a minute or two before he moved forward enough to allow other people to get by.

A minute or two seems like a long time for us to wait.

———◇※◇———

Nothing: NOTHING is worse for humanity than to get in line at the grocery store behind the person who needs a price check, but there I was behind Mr. Pasta-Won't-Scan. So I waited while the cashier flagged down a carry-out (or a bagger if you live in New England). I waited while the carry-out went for the item. I waited while the cashier chatted with the man. I waited while she finished ringing him up.

And I waited patiently.

This should be an Olympic sport, because it is so physical. If curling can qualify, then I think the skill of waiting deserves a shot. Consider the act of slowing your breathing and loosening your shoulders. Think about the control it takes to keep your fingers and toes from tapping. Then there is the muscle discipline of smiling instead of squinching your lips together. And resisting the urge to sigh loudly almost requires Lamaze training. Finally, one must be able to smile through the eyes. Through the eyes, I tell you, and communicate to the cashier, when she looks at you apologetically, that it's okay. And mean it.

Do you know how grueling the physical exertion of sincerity is?

Finally, it was my turn in line, and the cashier said, "Sorry about the wait."

"It's okay. I'm in no hurry," I said.

I am in no hurry. It's a statement of choice that's a gift of grace to the people around us.

CHAPTER FOURTEEN

TAMING THIS TONGUE

When I was in grade school, if someone threw up, the janitor would spread this sawdust-looking stuff on it to absorb the liquid. (I wonder who invented such a product.) All the kids would walk a wide circle around the throw-up, looking at it, but staying as far away as possible.

This chapter is my throw-up chapter, and it makes me a little sick to write it. I wish someone could throw that sawdust stuff on this area of my life, absorbing all the yuck and all the regret.

Here's the thing: I do words. I've always loved to speak and write and read. These are gifts I have used to build up the body of Christ, and I use them now, as I reach out to you with this message of hope about your potential to be blameless.

But in my words also lie my greatest moments of shame.

It was a short email, maybe three sentences, but it never occurred to me how it would sound when it came to his ears. So I found myself in our pastor's office, and all he could say to begin with was, "Wow, Christy."

Immediately, I saw the offense, but it was too late to retract it. I apologized. He graciously forgave me. But damage was done. Matt was on a mission trip to Belize at the time, so I found myself alone to deal with my humiliation. I couldn't take a full breath for the embarrassment of it, and I wondered how I could possibly be in this place again.

"Again" is the most appalling word.

Over seven hundred blog posts have been published from this computer since 2012. Matt is a counter, so

I made him do the math. If each blog post averages four hundred words and a book on the shelf averages thirty-five thousand words, how many books have I written, if I compile all my blog posts behind cover pages? Eight books.

Ten books, if you count how many times I've gotten out of bed at midnight, walked downstairs, and deleted a blog post because I thought it was stupid or offensive, or stupid *and* offensive. Probably it wasn't, but at midnight I tend to think I'm the worst writer ever.

So let's say eight books, and all of them claiming to help my readers get to know God. All of these words lifting up the good news of Jesus, and trying to encourage the precious souls of people. Words to help people understand the magnificent promises of God. Words to help people persevere through the darkest of times. Words to help people know they are loved.

But from this same computer, the very same keyboard, I kept sending out emails and Facebook messages that were thoughtless and hurtful. How was that possible?

In the same day I would get a note from a reader: How my words were just what she needed to hear from the Lord that day. And then an email from a friend: How could I say those things that cut her to the heart?

James writes about this very problem in his letter to believers in Christ: "From the same mouth come blessing and cursing. My brothers, these things ought not to be so" (James 3:10).

Except I'm thinking, *James, you have NO IDEA!* When James wrote his letter, he could not imagine a world with email and texting: people sending words back and forth in split seconds, without the advantage of body language to elicit instant apologies and rephrasing of words to avoid hurt feelings.

But obviously, James was speaking prophetically about my tongue. Night after night, I have gone to bed asking myself, *Why in the world did you say that to that person?*

⁂

One day I found myself writing an email to someone, and from my peripheral vision, I could see my husband walking down the stairs. Before he got to me, I had closed out of the email I was writing. That was when I knew I had a profound problem. I felt like a woman with a flask of liquor I was trying to shove into the desk drawer before my husband could see I was drinking AGAIN. Except in my case it was words

I was trying to hide. Words I shouldn't be saying to someone, but Just. Couldn't. Stop.

I think my ministry of writing had me slowly climbing to a lofty perch within my soul. *See me way up here? See how I have all this Bible knowledge and how you should listen to me because of my great wisdom?*

But when that "great wisdom" needed to be minimized on the screen before my husband could see it? Danger.

DEFCON 5.

She made me upset, and I had a hard time communicating with her in person, so I sat down to write a long email. Really long. I was articulate and well-spoken, detailing her offenses with great clarity. Because I am a good writer.

Then I hit "send."

Her long email came back to me, and I found myself more upset. So I wrote back with well-spoken words that hit a target, and I thought I was "working things out" with her, but really I was firing arrows, each email a little sharper than the last, until I had inflicted a great wound in the name of communication, a wound that never fully healed.

I was ashamed.

I had worked for the transcription company for a few years, but then they made some huge changes that made my job impossible. Before, I had always been assigned to type reports for certain doctors, but now they were putting us in a queue, and I never knew what doctor I would get. To learn a new doctor's voice is like learning a foreign language for every report. It became impossible.

So I sat down and wrote quite an email voicing my complaints loud and clear.

Send.

That week, I received a letter in the mail from my company. I was being let go, and the letter gave me instructions for my termination. I called Matt, who was at work. Sobbing from a fetal position on our bedroom floor, I couldn't even tell him the problem over the phone. He flew home in a panic, thinking I was bleeding out or something. When he walked into the bedroom, I reached up, handed him the letter and told him what I had done.

He talked me off the ledge, encouraging me to call the company.

When I pulled myself together, I called and found out that the letter had been sent in error to several people. I was not terminated. It had nothing to do with the email I had sent them. But this was a red flag, showing how bad my problem with impetuous communication was. Would I never change?

I had been hiding my email problem from my husband for a long time, minimizing emails when he would come near my computer, but one day I again sent something that hurt someone. It was the last straw, and I realized I needed help.

Hello, my name is Christy Fitzwater, and I speak and write without thinking.

Hello, Christy Fitzwater.

Jesus sent in the cavalry to help me, and his name is Matthew Fitzwater. He was, until then, an untapped resource. But I went upstairs and, in painful humility, told my husband I had a problem. He gave me advice that changed my life, and I realized he could have helped me all along, if I had only confessed my sin to him and asked for help earlier.

Husbands are heroes who just don't remember to pick up their socks.

About a month ago I planned a women's night at our church, and I asked five colorful women, of all different personalities and in all different stages of life, to be in a panel discussion on self-control. At some point, every single one of them mentioned that her husband was the voice of reason in her life, encouraging her to slow down or say "no" more often, or providing other wise counsel. Giving us husbands may be Jesus' greatest show of power in helping us become blameless women.

So I poured out my heart to my husband, and he had answers.

First, he told me that the computer is for broadcasting to large audiences and NOT for serious personal communications. If I had something wise to say, I needed to be able to say it to a broad range of people. If I had something personal to say to someone, it needed to be face-to-face, in front of the living, breathing human being. No emails about anything personal allowed.

Do you know how helpful it was to be given parameters?

He also got a big notecard, on which he wrote: "Who is going to read this, and how is it going to make them feel?" I tacked it to the corkboard that hangs over my computer.

We have a friend who smoked for years, and he says one day God just took that desire away from him. He hasn't smoked a cigarette since. My story is dramatic like that. I immediately stopped writing any personal emails. Now I always look at Matt's question, and I blame him for many of my deleted blog posts. In the middle of the night, I will wake up and think, "That's a really great post, but if this friend reads it, she will feel like I'm pointing to her."

Delete, delete, delete.

I used to secretly despise James for saying, "No human being can tame the tongue. It is a restless evil, full of deadly poison" (James 3:8). I used to read that statement and think there was no hope for me to ever, ever get my tongue under control. But now I know that in the same Bible, there is the word "blameless" written for me, because "He chose us in him before the foundation of the world, that we should be holy and blameless before him" (Ephesians 1:4).

God has always intended for me to speak only words that bring Him glory.

No man can tame the tongue, but God can. Aha! What a great discovery this is. And God put my husband as head over our household for a reason, to help this wife get her words under control. Submission to my husband's authority was the life preserver God threw out to this drowning woman, and I am so thankful.

--------◦──⟡⟐⟡──◦--------

In the year after my dad went to be with the Lord, I drove the twelve-hour stretch of highway many times to visit my mom. On one of those trips, I downloaded the audio version of *Anne of Green Gables*, by Louisa May Alcott, to listen to on the way. God encouraged my heart so much as I listened to that story.

Like Anne, I have so many words. In fact, when I got back from Wyoming, my husband was amazed at how long I could talk about my enjoyment of *Anne of Green Gables*. "Are you really talking to me about that book again?" he asked. And I decided he was my own Matthew Cuthbert, who just listens and listens and listens, until he has what my mom calls "cauliflower ear." (I think it's weird that my un-athletic mom uses a wrestling term, but whatever.)

As I listened to the story of Anne, though, I could see myself in her. Her impetuous words got her in trouble on more than one occasion, and when she became proficient at apologizing to people because of so much practice, I sympathized with her. But her words were also what everyone loved about her, and she could hold an audience spellbound with her stories.

At one point in the story, when Anne has gotten older, Marilla mentions that Annehas changed from the chatty, impetuous little girl she used to be.

"I'm not a bit changed – not really," Anne replies. "I'm only just pruned down and branched out."

This is the work God does as He brings us into blameless living. We are beautiful creations of His, made in His image, and we just need to be pruned down so we can branch out.

It was a Friday at school, and I was tired and had a cold. I wasn't in the mood to be gracious and lenient, and the boys in the back were chatting while I was trying to explain something. "I'm losing patience with you guys," I said. "I'm tired of how you're always checking out while I'm trying to teach." I humiliated them in front of all their peers.

So last night I was awake because of my cold, and because of the misery of those words I spoke. As I blew my nose five hundred times, I sank down into hopelessness. *Lord, will I never be able to control this tongue of mine?*

But then I remembered this book I'm writing about becoming blameless. While I hope you're enjoying it, you need to know that this book God has me writing is really my personal journal of transformation.

As I thought about that encounter with my students, I realized that I should have talked to them privately if I was upset at them, instead of in front of the whole class. I've noticed that God seems to work hard to maintain my dignity while He does this pruning of my soul, so shouldn't I return that favor to my students?

Next, I needed to keep plugging away at controlling my tongue, and trusting that God was going to finish the work He started in me.

I have hope, because it has always been God's intention for me to be blameless with my words.

CHAPTER FIFTEEN

CURSE GOD?

The first time it happened, we were living in the old yellow house on Third Avenue East. Our friend had convinced us that it was an excellent time to build, and that we should follow his family into a beautiful young subdivision and build there, too. I loved our little yellow house and was scared at the thought of trying to sell it and tackle the job of having a house built. So I awoke in the middle of the night, filled with anxiety, and couldn't go back to sleep.

Night after night, the sleeplessness continued, and I was Jacob wrestling with the angel of insomnia. Frustrated at being so tired and yet so wide awake, I would lie in bed and toss and turn. The tears would fall, and I would find myself angry and screaming the question at God a hundred times a night: *Why won't You help me sleep?* The morning would come, and I would walk like a zombie through the day, trying to have enough energy to be a mom, but needing an afternoon nap more than my children did.

I was so frustrated with God, and I felt frustrated that I was frustrated. The story of Job came to mind, because I felt like my life was that horrible. Mentally, I was overhearing Job's conversation with his wife. As they talked about the trauma they were experiencing, she spewed angry words at him: "Do you still hold fast your integrity? Curse God and die."

Job replied, "You speak as one of the foolish women would speak. Shall we receive good from God, and shall we not receive evil?" (Job 2:9-10).

The foolish woman wanted him to throw away his integrity. In my insomnia, I had arrived at the same decision: curse God and carry the shame of that curse, or accept the sleepless nights and be able to hold my head up before the Almighty. As I tossed and turned in the night, the curse was on the tip of my tongue, but I did not want to be ashamed.

One night I said, *Okay, Lord.* Two words of submission that changed everything.

I still couldn't sleep. Most nights I would wake up around two or three o'clock and finally decide to get up for a short time, to try to shift mental gears. After an hour or two, I would lie back down and pray, *Lord, You decide whether I sleep or not in this night. Please grant me sleep, but if You don't, I still say You are good to me.*

A dozen years later, insomnia is still the norm for me, but I make the choice to carry no shame in the night by how I respond to it.

When my husband came home from Africa with a chronic ailment several years ago, and my life was jerked into a care-giving role, I was once again faced with the temptation to curse God for the circumstance in which we found ourselves. How was it possible that my husband could go to Africa to do good, and be rewarded with debilitating physical problems? Why would God do this to our family?

Once again, I could see the fire in the eyes of Job's wife. I could see the pain of grief slumping her shoulders, and the anger at God that caused her to throw up her hands in front of Job. Her children were all dead. Her husband was sick. The financial loss was unbearable.

"Do you still hold fast your integrity? Curse God and die," she said.

Would I talk like this foolish woman? Or would I hold on to my integrity? Would I open my hands and accept this illness from God, as if it were a gift from Him to be received?

There came a day when Matt read the online stories of others who were suffering with the same reactions to the medication he had taken as an anti-malarial treatment. That same week, he went to the doctor, who shook his head and said, "Yes. Yes, this is most likely what you're experiencing."

In that week, I squared my shoulders in front of the Lord and prayed, *I will not be ashamed in front of You. I will not curse You.* And I pulled up those two words that had saved me from going crazy on sleepless nights. The only two words you can get out sometimes, when life is so hard: *Okay, Lord.*

In that year, I lived out Lemony Snicket's book, *A Series of Unfortunate Events.* The unfortunate events began with an answer to prayer in August of 2013. Because of changes in the health care system, my medical transcription job had phased out earlier in the year, and while I was hoping we could make it on Matt's pastoral salary, that simply wasn't the case. I started praying for a job in which I could work later in the day, given my insomnia. And I prayed for a job that would allow me to pursue my writing in the mornings.

My husband went to breakfast with some friends, and asked one of them how his new job as principal was going.

He replied, "Fine, except I'm in desperate need of a Spanish teacher."

That was eight o'clock in the morning, and by noon I had interviewed and was shaking hands on the job. It was two weeks until school would start.

I had never taught Spanish, and it had been twenty years since I had studied Spanish in college. Living in northern Montana had allowed me zero opportunities to use or improve my language skills, so I walked into that job as green and unprepared as a teacher could be.

In October, our dog developed a cancerous leg tumor that started oozing. (I can hear my husband saying, "Please don't say 'oozing.'") We took our eleven-year-old black lab to the vet, and I had to see my husband's face as they took our dog away, to return to us no more. When I went to school an hour later, I took my students outside to play soccer in the sun. I was too upset to teach a Spanish lesson.

During the Thanksgiving holiday, our daughter's boyfriend asked if he could meet privately to talk to Matt about something. We knew. My husband came home with eyes glazed over, having given permission for our daughter to marry this wonderful boy. We were so happy for her, but spent the entire holiday looking at each another over the top of her head, and getting teary. In December, she said yes and accepted the sparkly on her finger, and we hugged. Then I went someplace private and had a very large panic attack. Okay, so I was going to plan Spanish lessons and a wedding. Breathe into the paper bag. Breathe.

We started looking at Pinterest boards, and I started making lists that seemed impossible. Wedding notebook on one counter. Spanish lesson plans on another.

Then it was February 15, and my husband preached the sermon that night, telling about how God had comforted him when his dad had passed away some two decades before. I got home after church and set my Bible down on the counter. The phone rang, and it was my brother and my mom.

"Chris, we have to tell you something," Arie said. I

could hear the news before he said it.

"I was snowmobiling with dad today," said my brother. "He slumped over on his machine. And he died. He died today."

And in that one moment I could see Job's wife. She was too far away for me to hear her, but I could read her lips. *Curse God and die*, she said. *Curse Him.*

But I could hear my conversation with Dad at the grocery story coffee shop just two months before this phone call. Him with coffee, black. Me with a small mocha, single shot.

"I hope I never get sick and need care," he said in his gruff Wyoming-man voice. "If I ever get sick, you just take me into the woods and drop me off. Just drop me off and leave me. I don't wantcha to hafta take care of me."

"Oh, Dad," I laughed.

And in the second after my brother said, "Dad died," I turned my back on Job's wife, and all I could think was how good and kind God was. How good and kind to let my dad die in the woods. I thought, *Well Dad, there ya go. Just like you wanted*, and I couldn't help but laugh. In that moment, I couldn't help but be so happy for him and so happy with God.

And I decided I was going to grieve with my head up. I was going to accept this trouble from God and not have reason to be ashamed at my response to the pain.

How could I curse the Lord when he had honored Dad's request in this way? How could I curse God when all these friends kept coming by and hugging me and crying with me? How could I curse God when my cousin wrapped his big old frame around me and squeezed me so tight?

So much love.

I was not going to be ashamed in how I grieved. I write these words when it is only a week until the one-year anniversary of my dad going to be with the Lord. I can look back over the year and see how close God came to me and to my family. God is good.

Oh, how I wish I could say that was the end of the trouble. In the same month my dad died, I figured out we owed a big chunk of taxes that consumed all of my daughter's wedding money and then some. My friend of many years and I parted ways. I was almost not re-hired for my job because I had floundered so much in the first year. They did give me another chance, but oh, the humiliation. And then the sweet pain of seeing my daughter walk down the aisle and leave our home, as I sat next to my mother who grieved that my dad was not there to see the wedding. Trial upon trial.

I sobbed into the pillow more nights than I can count during this series of unfortunate events, but I have not put my head on that pillow with shame in front of my God. He has helped me not to be angry with Him. He has always meant for me to be blameless, and I have found Him to be at work toward this end, even in grief and on hard, hard days. He has helped me cling to Him instead of pounding fists against His chest.

The young woman sat in front of me at church, and shared with me how lost she was in this season of her life. She had so many things she hoped to be and do for God, yet she felt like nothing was happening and God was not taking her anywhere.

"Do you ever feel angry with God," she asked?

"No, I said firmly. "No, I will not let myself be angry at God."

Because there is shame in cursing God when He allows pain and hard times to come our way. There is shame in being so weak in our faith, when we should be strong and trusting Him. There is shame in doubting His love and grace when it passes behind a cloud for a time.

And God intends for us to blameless in front of Him, which means holding tight to our faith, even when the hurricane winds of trial try to rip it from our hands. What joy He has in us, and what joy we have Him in when we have held on tight.

CHAPTER SIXTEEN

―――――✦―――――

THE QUESTION OF LOYALTY

Yesterday morning, my quiet time with God was perfection. With a cozy quilt spread across my lap, and a steaming cup of coffee in hand, I opened my Spanish Bible and began to read Psalm 15. Using all my great skills of meditation, I pondered each verse and prayed that the Lord would develop in me the qualities I was reading about.

I confessed my weakness and inability to create the character traits I was seeing in this psalm. I thanked God for the transforming presence and power of Jesus in my soul. *Change me Lord. Let this list of character traits describe who I am.*

I especially meditated on one verse: "He whose walk is blameless...keeps an oath even when it hurts" (Psalm 15:1,4 NIV). After a long time of prayer, I serenely closed the Bible and went upstairs to kiss Matt goodbye before he left for work.

"I just realized that I double-booked myself," Matt said. In order to keep an appointment he had made, he was going to have to cancel the bike ride he had planned with our son. Our son, who would be graduating in a few months and leaving for Texas to attend a university.

I had a cow. Three cows.

I whipped around, angry, and did what I always do when I'm upset: dive into housework, with my back turned to that man. But then Psalm 15 came to mind. While scrubbing with undue effort, I had to admit to myself that I was impressed that Matt would keep his first commitment, when I knew I would have canceled if I were in his shoes.

I also felt his hurt. I felt how much it hurt both of us, for him to have to bow out on the second plan with our son, in order to keep the first. But I couldn't get the psalmist's words out of my mind: *A blameless man keeps his oath.*

Matt gave me a quick kiss, but I could feel his emotional distance. When I looked at his face, he was white as a ghost.

Pain.

I could see the pain it was causing him to keep his commitment.

"You're right," I said, at great expense. "You're right. You have to keep your promise to the first person."

Matt left the house ashen, with the pain of my response added to the guilt he was already feeling about his error in scheduling. The second he got to church, he was calling me, at the same time I had hit "send" on a text explaining my quiet-time meditation on Psalm 15:4. I apologized for my anger, and added, "You're a good man." A good man keeps his oath, even when it hurts.

I wonder if the Lord had raised His eyebrows that morning, while I took another sip of my coffee and thought about His words. I wonder what look He had on His face when I was begging Him to grow those character traits in me. *Okay, kid. Let's see if you can put your money where your mouth is.*

I did. I finally submitted to the truth of Psalm 15:4, but it was an ugly trip to get there. Obedience is death to what we want. A bloody death of self will. Anyone can sip coffee and read the Bible, but if we want to become blameless, we have to be willing to believe and act on whatever truth God shows us in His words.

God doesn't give written tests, only tests of

demonstration.

I was in the church kitchen, serving up hot dogs for a celebration. One of our pastor friends walked up, holding his sweet baby girl in one arm. I smiled at the pacifier that was clipped to his shirt front and admired his choice of accessories.

"I sure wish your husband could go to Canada with me," he said.

Matt had called me the day before, and asked what I thought about him traveling up to Canada with this pastor friend of ours, to take a one-week intensive class at the seminary there. The class would take place during the week before our son's graduation, but I valued this opportunity for Matt to improve his craft of preaching, and encouraged him to go for it. Told him we would manage.

Later that day, Matt overheard me talking to someone on the phone about a graduation I would be attending during the week he would be gone. It was the graduation of our dear friend's son.

"That settles it," he said. "I'm not going to Canada."

"Why?" I asked.

"There's no way I'm going to miss that graduation."

As I was talking to my friend, me with a hot dog in my hand, and him with the pacifier dangling from his shirt, he said, "Matt's really loyal, isn't he?"

"Yes. Yes, he is," I said. I confessed that I tend to make decisions based on what's good for me, rarely making sacrifices out of loyalty to someone else, but I'm trying to grow in this.

He nodded, considering my words.

"Yeah," he said.

My son was exhausted, and my mother's heart went out to him. It was a Saturday, and he had just finished a week full of events, late nights, and hours logged at work. But his team was doing some yard work that morning as a fundraiser for their summer mission trip.

"Do you think I could just bow out on this one, mom?" he said. "I'm so tired."

I looked at his eyes, which were puffy with fatigue. With every ounce of my being, I wanted to go tuck him into bed. My thought was, *He should rest!*

But God had been working in my heart. He was teaching me about loyalty, so what normally would have been an answer focused on self-preservation came out like this instead: "What about your team? What will you be saying to them if they all work, and you stay home in bed?"

These were not old-Christy words. These were new, something foreign and good being spurred on by the Spirit of God inside me. I thought about how my lack of loyalty had bubbled over onto my children all these years. So many times I had encouraged them to do what was good for them, without considering how it would affect others. But I suppose God can change a mom's heart even when she's forty-six, and her boy is seventeen.

"You're right," he said.

A blameless man keeps his word, even when it hurts.

He dragged himself out the door, and worked hard that morning. Later, we got a note from the team leader, saying that we should be proud of our son and the contribution he had made to the team.

I was starting to understand that loyalty is a good choice.

I don't normally read books more than once, but when I was at my mother-in-law's one day, I reached for Dee Henderson's O'Malley Series for the umpteenth time. (I think "umpteenth" is a word someone made up because they were embarrassed to say the actual amount of times they had done something.) It's her characters that draw me in, and I think that's because she has sketched seven people who are fiercely loyal to each other. They are orphans who grew up together, and have taken on the same last name in order to be a family. They know they can call each other at any time of night and get a listening ear. They have pagers with an emergency number for each sibling, and if the emergency number shows up, the whole family drops everything and comes to the rescue.

I want to be like them, but I know I am not there yet.

The previous day had been thirty-six hours long. I had slept only about four hours in the night and then left the house at 7:50 to go to an adoption hearing for our friends. (Okay, so there is some loyalty in me.) From there, I went to the school, where I worked all morning planning for the next year. I taught in the afternoon, and then ran some errands with my husband. From there, I raced home and made "superhero green" Rice

Crispy treats, to take to the adoption party at church. There I stood in the kitchen for a few hours, serving up a few hundred hot dogs and hamburgers.

The next morning, I woke up with a horrible headache, feeling exhausted into my bones. All I wanted was to sip coffee and stay in bed with a book for the day.

But I had clicked "join" on the Facebook evite the week prior, promising I would come to the birthday party for our friend's little girl, who was turning one. My habit of self-preservation kicked in, and I thought, *I'm going to text them and say I just can't make it.* I knew they would understand how tired I was. It wouldn't be a big deal.

But the Holy Spirit used the O'Malley characters to do some work in my heart.

The O'Malley siblings would never say they were going to a party and then not show up just because they were tired.

He whose walk is blameless keeps his oath even when it hurts.

So I went.

And that was the sign of a big change in me. I was making a decision based on my loyalty to another person, instead of my own self-centered need. I was laying down my life for someone else, and it felt momentous.

The family who had adopted the little boy the day before – they were at this birthday party. This family has demonstrated loyalty to me for years, but it stood out to me even more on this day. Their previous day had been just as long, and surely more emotionally taxing than it had been for me. But they had said they would come to this birthday party, and they did.

I sat down next to my sister-in-law while we watched little Hazel open her birthday presents. My sister-in-law had helped plan and carry out the adoption party the night before, and she was as tired as I was.

"I thought about not coming to this birthday party," she said. "But I said I would come. I really want to be a woman of my word."

Yes. Yes, me too.

I am amazed that God would start this new work in the heart of a grown woman. Some folks say that you can't teach an old dog new tricks, and I could use that as an excuse for not changing my habit of self-preservation. But God is making me into a new person. I'm getting older, but I see Him doing more transformation in me than ever before.

CHAPTER SEVENTEEN

You're Just the Right Age

It was the end of 2014, and Pinterest sent me a personal message (because they really care about me) suggesting I create a 2015 board. I had just been watching podcasts by Michael Hyatt about the importance of setting challenging goals with do-able action points for the new year, so I was already primed to set my own goals.

In the kitchen, I had an informal meeting with my twenty-year-old daughter, whom I consider to be my personal assistant in all things, and asked her to help me name the Pinterest board.My girl is a quiet, reserved person, but she will tell me the truth. I kept throwing out name ideas, and she kept giving me the slow head shake. Finally, she suggested "Vision 2015," and that was perfect. So let it be written. So let it be done.

We have an ancient hot-air popper that I pull out every once in a while for movie night. My husband, a mature pastor in his mid-forties, becomes eight years old when I turn it on. He hops around and gets all excited when the popcorn starts popping and growing up out of the machine and spilling into the bowl. Then comes a very generous helping of butter and salt, for which I will not apologize. That image is all I can think of to describe to you how I felt, as I sat down in front of the computer to create Vision 2015 (cue trumpets playing).

These goals I was about to make were popping and growing up out of my soul, hardly to be contained. They started as kernels of shame in years past, and with the heat of the Son they were becoming something celebratory and joyful and deserving of butter.

"Hurry! Get a big bowl under here!" my husband says. "It's coming!"

In 1 John 3:1, John says, "See what kind of love the Father has given to us, that we should be called children of God; and so we are." And then John speaks twice to the children of God about what they will be.

"What we will be has not yet appeared." Don't we know it? We're not there yet. We fail at things every day. We know we fall short without John bringing it up. "But we know that when he appears we shall be like him" (1 John 3:2).

Sometimes you just need to say "We shall," because it carries more weight in old English. And haven't I been whispering this truth for chapters and chapters now?

We shall be blameless.

We shall be pure.

When you're forty-something and about to turn the calendar to 2015, with your birthday coming up right away, you can look back and see how God has been purifying your life. You can see it.

John says, "And everyone who thus hopes in him purifies himself as he is pure" (1 John 3:3). I'm starting to see how my goals for 2015 are popping up, and up, and up, because of hope. Because of Christ working in me, there is hope that I can be pure, and all that hope is going to spill into the new year.

Somebody get a bowl!

My friend is an artist at his core, so he really gets

me. Although his medium is a guitar and computer graphics, and mine is Word documents and a website, we think the same. He is a pastor who works alongside my husband, and he and his wife and baby girl joined us at my mother-in-law's house on Christmas Day.

My mother-in-law thought maybe we should go light, and just have appetizers to snack on for the day, instead of a big Christmas dinner. She is a southern woman, though, so every inch of her kitchen bar was covered with food, and we could have invited Cox's army to join us and sent them home with leftovers.

I found myself filling yet another plate with cheese and crackers and meatballs (you can see where the Vision 2015 goal of working out came into play here.) Pastor Andy joined me at the food bar, while the nephews played Leapster® in the back room and everyone else watched football.

"So how's the whole book thing coming?" he asked.

I told him about my emails back and forth with the publisher, and how I was hoping for a book contract for my birthday. I got all excited about this new stage of my life, with empty nest only a few months away, but this new writing work blossoming in front of me. I was overflowing with the joy of God working through this heart of mine to write something meaningful for other people.

He talked about his music, and how some of his dreams were starting to come alive. He was mentoring young people to be passionate worship leaders, and I could see in his eyes what I felt in my own heart. Could we possibly use our art to make a difference in this world?

It's scary to speak the dreams out loud, as if saying them will make the bubble pop and disappear.

"Umm, not to offend you," he said. Then he looked like he was thinking better of his words.

I encouraged him to keep going, to say what he was thinking.

"Not to offend you, but it gives me a lot of hope that your dreams are just getting going...at your age."

"Yes," I replied, un-offended. "They're just getting going. My life is just starting," I said to this young man who is more than a decade behind me.

My life is just starting.

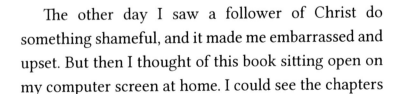

The other day I saw a follower of Christ do something shameful, and it made me embarrassed and upset. But then I thought of this book sitting open on my computer screen at home. I could see the chapters piling up, my own journey filling page after page.

"I think everyone should have to write a book about how God has brought them out of shame," I told my husband.

Having my own journey so fresh in my mind filled me with grace toward this follower of Christ who had messed up, and I could hear Paul saying, in Ephesians 1:4, that we were chosen in Christ to be holy and blameless.

I could see my friend's future blamelessness. I could see the heat on the kernels and could imagine his holiness popping up, up, up and into the bowl.

Lord, purify this fellow traveler, I prayed. *You will, I know You will.*

And you.

I'm smiling warmly at you, if you could only see it. There is so much hope for your life. At your age.

In the same letter in which Paul tells the followers of Christ they were chosen to be blameless, he says, "For we are his workmanship, created in Christ Jesus for good works, which God prepared beforehand, that we should walk in them" (Ephesians 2:10). So much advance work has been done for your life.

Advance planning for your blamelessness.

Advance planning for you to do good work.

And the two are twisted together. God works in our hearts, by the millimeters most often, purifying and purifying us. In little bits at a time, He removes the shame and the lies, replacing them with holiness and truth. One day at a time, we get closer to *being* the person God always intended us to be, which allows us to get closer to *doing* what He has always intended us to do. He plants dreams inside of us, so we start thinking of how we can change the world for the sake of His name, and He purifies our hearts so we can do those dreams.

———✦✦✦———

I went to the funeral of a woman who was in her mid-eighties. Someone read from the thesis paper they had found on her desk, because she had recently gotten her bachelor's in Biblical studies and was working on her master's. She was following hard after God, and I think she thought her life was just getting started. At the end of the funeral service, by her request, a trio of ladies sang the Disney song, "Zip-a-Dee-Doo-Dah." I laughed out loud, and left the funeral humming the lyrics to that song.

I don't mean any disrespect to the Apostle Paul, but I can picture him humming that song, trying to tell us that we are people who have hope. Hope of *blameless* and *holy*. Hope of doing good work for the kingdom. Hope of becoming everything God ever intended us to be. There's plenty of sunshine coming our way.

You can make every effort to purify your life, in the kitchen and the checkbook and the relationships, and in all the other veins of your life, because Jesus came to make purity a reality for you.

Look at what Jesus has done in my life, and be assured that we can be people who rest our heads on the pillow at night, feeling good about who we are and how we are living.

And whatever age your driver's license says is the perfect age to get started.

ABOUT THE AUTHOR

Christy Fitzwater is a simple Wyoming girl who, in middle school, asked God if someday she might please write Bible studies for people. She attended the University of Mary Hardin-Baylor, in central Texas, where she met a tall Montana man and agreed to move north with him permanently. Using her English degree and love for Bible truth, she began writing children's Bible lessons for the kids at church and then small group Bible study guides for teenagers and adults. From there she began blogging, at her daughter's suggestion, and she has found great joy in writing short devotionals online. Her goal is to help people get to a place where they can brag that they know God and to live the big, meaningful life God has planned for them. These days Christy considers it romantic to run alongside her husband–doing God's kingdom work in Big Sky Country, as he preaches good news and she writes about it. Find Christy's devotional writing and Bible-teaching newsletters at christyfitzwater.com.

CPSIA information can be obtained at www.ICGtesting.com
Printed in the USA
LVOW07s0309070616

491405LV00009B/375/P